MARTIAL ARTS: Learn How to Become The Ultimate Warrior

By Robert Zangari, Founder of Ryu Zangari Do

Disclaimer: Please note that the Publisher and Author of this book are NOT RESPONSIBLE in any manner whatsoever for any injury that may result from practicing the techniques and/or following the instructions given within. Martial Arts training can be dangerous – both to you and to others – if not practiced safely and correctly. If you're in doubt consult with a trained Martial Arts Professional before beginning. Before performing any physical exercise or training program outlined in this book consult your physician prior to your training.

Published by RZD Academy of Martial Arts & Life
Layton, Utah
www.Martial-Arts-RZDAcademy.com

Printed by Lulu
3131 Hillsborough Street
Raleigh, North Carolina

Copyright 2010, RZD Academy of Martial Arts & Life

ISNB – 10: 0615354831

ISBN – 13: 978-0-615-35483-5

Cover design – Robert Zangari & Marina Lukach of www.foto-domik.com.ua

Table Contents

About the Author 8

Acknowledgements 9

Introduction 10

Chapter One 11

   Street Fighting 12

      Preset Rigidity in situations 14

      Emotions 15

      Mindset 18

   A Darker Side to Things 19

Chapter Two 23

   End a fight quick! 24

      Speed - 25

      Agility - 25

      Power - 25

      Firm wits - 26

      Iron Determination - 27

   You need an "Offensive Defense" 27

   Stealth in your actions is critical for victory 31

   Mindset is more important than skill and strength 37

   Expect Deception 38

   "Broken Rhythm" 38

   The Voice is often mightier than the Fist 40

   A Fit novice is better than an out of shape master 49

      Diet - 51

- Supplements - 52
- Flexibility - 53
- Strength Training - 53
- Weight Training - 54
- Cardiovascular 55
- Technique Training 55
- Everything is a Weapon 56
- Becoming their worst nightmare 58
- Three Steps to Perfection 59

Chapter Three 65
- Physical Requirements 67
  - Flexibility 67
  - Strength 68
  - Endurance 71
- Training Program 72
  - Day One 72
  - Day Two 73
- Fuel – The Life Blood of your Training 74
- Products 78
  - Nitric Oxide 79
  - Omega 3s and Tocotrinels 80
  - Muscle Repair Formulas 81
- Daily Inspiration 82

Chapter Four 85
- Words and Thoughts 86

Thought Projection	93
Mental Penetration	95
Trancing	99
Chapter Five	**103**
Ground Combat	104
Study your surroundings	106
Detach, mental bungee jumping	109
Mindset for combat, split personality	111
Preparation…	111
Actual Use…	112
Attack the weapons	115
Joint locks, breaks, and dislocations	116
Multiple Attackers	117
Disarming	122
Switching Styles	122
Be relentless	123
Multiple Strikes, Double, Triple and Quadruple	125
Double Strike	125
Triple Strike	126
Quadruple Strike	126
Chapter Six	**129**
The Mantra	130
The Effect of Music	131
Every time you strike you strike with a declaration	133
Visualize yourself as the winner every time	133

When you're tired, be your own Personal Drill Sergeant. 133

Have an "I can do it!" attitude.. 136

A Warrior's Spirit, Ken-Ki.. 137

Chapter Seven 139

    Meditation 140

    Mental Sparring.. 143

    Trance Development 145

    Mind Expansion 146

Chapter Eight 149

    Shadow Sparring 150

    Blind Fold Sparring 151

    Night time sparring without light 152

    Iron Shirt Training a.k.a. Pain Tolerance Training 154

        Hot & Cold 155

        Fire Exposure - 156

        Training on Hard Ground 157

        Everyday Training 158

    Emotional Control 158

Chapter Nine 161

The Standard, the Code.. 162

    Attributes and Personal Characteristics... 164

        Righteousness 165

        Virtue 165

        Honesty 165

        Loyalty.. 166

Benevolence 166
Patience 166
Diligence 166
Courage 167
Hope 167
Faith 167
Obedience 168
Kindness 168
Tenderness 168
Love 169
Gratitude 169
Respect 170
Conclusion 171
Bibliography 174

About the Author

Robert Zangari is a Professional Martial Arts Instructor. He has been a Martial Artist since 1994, and an Instructor since 2001. He is the founder of RZD Academy of Martial Arts & Life - a Martial Arts based Training and Personal Development Company that focuses on helping its students learn faster and more efficiently. www.Martial-Arts-RZDAcademy.com

Robert is the founder of "Ryu Zangari Do", a revolutionized system of fighting that combines his entire Martial Arts and Life experiences. www.Martial-Arts-RZDAcademy.com/RyuZangariDo

Robert has been trained in Karate, Wing Chun Gung Fu, Jeet Kune Do, Kenjutsu, Ninjutsu and To-Shin-Do.

Robert lives in Northern Utah with his wife and their three dogs

Outside of Martial Arts he enjoys Family activities, Architecture, Home Design, Reading, Jogging, Video Games (online and offline), and serving regularly in religious services.

Acknowledgements

I dedicate this book to my beloved daughter Kira. She helped motivate and inspire me to create this work. I also dedicate this book to my wonderful wife, without her this work could never have been completed.

I wish to thank everyone who has helped produce this work. I wish to thank my mentors, my editors and my colleagues. Thank you, may your Eternal God bless you forever and ever.

Introduction

Imagine yourself in the best physical, mental and spiritual condition. What are you like? Do you want to be there? Yes! Then let's start on a wonderful *Journey*! You obviously have some questions and have not found the answers yet, or you have and you want to compare you findings. Either way I can promise you will get whatever you are looking for.

This book is meant to be *interactional*. It is not a straight read. As you read, from time to time I will ask you some questions, so think about them, ponder them out in your mind and play it on your internal "Big Screen" – you've seen a big screen before right? You will find some *exercises* that will help you anchor your new found knowledge – *do them* right away and experience what you just read. You're going to learn some techniques for improving your skills, and ingraining things *quicker* and deeper into your mind, something we call at the Academy, ALTs - Accelerated Learning Techniques. These combinations of learning drastically speed up your learning ability not just for Martial Arts but anything, I mean ANYTHING in life! So go ahead and try it out on something else too, I dare you.

In this book you will find key principles that will shape not only the way you practice or teach Martial Arts, but your entire Life. This book is a compilation of years upon years of research, practice and experience; this book will save you time, effort and perhaps even some money. Now, let's get started!

Chapter One
The Real World

"Life is an ever growing battlefield."

The real world is completely different from the mat and for those who have been in tournaments and competitions know what I mean. Think about it, in the real world there are no limitations, no rules, no boundaries, no honor, and definitely no chivalry.

The world has changed over the past few hundred years, new philosophies introduced and blended together. Societies changed or collapsed. The rise of new technologies – certain things are ever changing, but there are also things that remain constant. Imagine two people fighting four hundred years ago, and compare it to a fight now. Yes their tools of combat are different, but the outcome is the same, *victory* or defeat.

Street Fighting

Street fighting is one of those ever changing things but yet constant. No one opponent is the same; no terrain is the same, not every situation is the same – but the outcome is the same every time, you *win* or you lose.

Now why do you (or if you haven't, will you) practice Martial Arts? Think about that for a second… for some as a sport, or self defense, or for another to gain greater discipline – no matter the reason, we must look back to what Martial Arts were made for, why did anyone ever invent these arts of fighting. To sum it up there are two reasons, to *conquer* and defend. Throughout time the art of fighting has been used ultimately for these two ends. Now what does the past have to do with the street? Well, some things change but others don't. That little part of the human mind to conquer or defend will always be there. The question is which side are *You* on?

Some methods have evolved in different ways; the Martial Arts of Asia have always been a way of discipline, protection, and enlightenment. The fighting styles of South America stemmed from ferociousness and secret warfare. The Knights of Europe held honor and protection above all. There are many different paths one might take along the *journey* to Martial perfection, and we will not cover them all in this book or this section.

Here is the question, where did this "street fighting" come from? We can look at it and see certain things in certain people; whether it be from a hard life growing up in a tough part of town, excessive crime, or underground challenge matches to test one's manhood. Those who fight on the street have a different aspect about them, fearlessness you could say, determination to win – it's something different than just practicing a kata in your local dojo.

EXAMPLE

Imagine this, in your mind compare two people, a teenager who grew up fighting on the street, and your average person who just completed his or her rank advancement to First Degree black belt (in whatever style, we won't point fingers at any particular style, and I'll explain the reason why in a minute). These two people met in a confrontation on the street, now in your mind imagine what it would be like, where are they, what do you see around them, is it a tight alley, a parking lot – whatever it may be set the stage. Before we act out this scenario lets out line a couple things. The new black belt has not had a confrontation like this, and for the other teenager this is just another day, nothing special. The Black Belt has only fought and trained on the mat, the street fighter fights in the streets and trains anywhere. As the fight plays out it starts quickly and ends quickly – who wins? The Street Fighter of course! Now why is that?

ANALYSIS

Preset Rigidity in situations

The real world is not like the mat. In a dojo or any other training place you;

- Have almost compliant sparring partners.
- You each know the same style.
- Fighting styles are almost identical because you have the same master or instructor; everyone is punching or kicking with the same form. It's all pretty uniform.
- In some schools certain combinations are drilled over and over, and in the mind of the student it's almost like a preset button on a phone.

For instance, you hit the number for the preset and it dials that phone number – you see a straight punch you block, parry, dodge or counter attack in a certain way. That's great for phones, but not in a street fight. There needs to be random unpredictability.

Think about it, if you had random unpredictability with your phone presets you would probably be mad when you hit the preset button to call your girlfriend/boyfriend and you got some Joe

Schmoe you don't even know. Wouldn't you go to your Phone Company and demand to get it fixed? Now compare that to a fight. If you are random in your patterns of attack, and completely unpredictable your opponent won't know what's hitting them, or when you're hitting them. The result, you *win*. Would you go complain to your instructor about that? Probably not. Preset patterns are great for phones but not in street fighting.

One of the Greatest Martial Artists of all time, Bruce Lee taught…

> "Be like water… when water flows into the cup, it becomes the cup. When water flows into the pot it becomes the pot… be like water".
>
> - Bruce Lee

Flexibility is one of the most important aspects in surviving a street fight. Not just the flexibility in your joints but in your strategies, your execution of strikes, grapples, defenses etc, and in dealing with the situation in ways other than fighting.

Emotions

The next great factor of why the black belt lost is Lack of Emotional Training. We train and train in the dojo or studio, rote drill after rote drill, making simulations of what a real world encounter would look like, but there's one thing that's missing – the emotion behind it.

In the dojo you have a sense of security, you feel safe being there. Face it, you wouldn't be there if you didn't feel comfortable. Security and the feelings of friendliness are key aspects in having an effective dojo. If you felt scared you wouldn't go. So I'm not saying that security is bad, it's good, but in training the fear on the battlefield needs to be simulated, not just the actions of defending yourself. Sometimes people who have never fought in an actual fight clam up, even with rank upon rank. They weren't taught to tame their fears and control their emotions.

One key component *implemented* in RZD Academy of Martial Arts & Life is *emotion* behind every Self Defense situation you learn. There is emotional backing to everything – behind your training partner's actions and your own. Imagine yourself training every time in deeply involved emotional experiences. You will learn how to correctly manage your emotions. Your skills will skyrocket, and actual results will be more worthwhile and satisfying, not to mention life saving.

Here's an experience from one of my mentors, Steven K. Hayes, in his book *The Ninja and their secret fighting art* he recounts a story of when he was training in Japan under Masaaki Hatsumi. Late one evening Steven, another student and Hatsumi Sensei were driving down a gravel road for a late night training session. After parking their vehicle they embarked on a journey to the local golf course. To his surprise Steven remarked they'd never be able do this in America, and Hatsumi Sensei replied you can't in Japan either. Each time Hatsumi Sensei would take his students on this type of night training it was always in a new environment, why? To keep up their ability of awareness, if it was rote it would defeat the purpose. They eventually ended up behind the ninth tee, where four others met up with them. They began their training session with unarmed combat. Steven recounts no matter how hard he hit he could not land a punch on his opponent, however once his perspective changed he was able to make out the silhouettes of the others against the stars. (Hayes, 1981)

Think about that - what emotions would be flowing? Its pitch black and you *can't see* punches and kicks flying at you. *Thoughts* of the security guard calling the police and being thrown in jail. You can't see the ground, you *don't know* if a sand trap is behind you or a tree to your side. Of course he eventually was able to see vaguely what was around him, but don't you think there was a *swelling of emotions* – Controlled or not? How would you feel if you were right there on that golf course? *Write* it down.

Now here's where the fun begins – don't go out to your local golf course and do this, I don't want the legal liability, so I'm telling you DO NOT DO IT! However, simulate something like this. *Remember* those emotions you just wrote down? Make them a reality with this exercise. Get together with some of the people you know who practice martial arts, take a night and go somewhere and have sparring matches in the dark – be safe and reasonable, but have a match or two in the nighttime and see how that differs from on the mat in your dojo.

Of course you will never be able to practice what it's like exactly, but it will definitely give you the training you need to calm your emotions and keep a cool head in an actual fight. Plus you will have a blast! I always enjoy my late night training sessions, and I'm sure you will too.

Mindset

The Greatest key to surviving on the street is your mindset. The street fighter has had plenty of time and experience to get it into his head that "I'm never going to lose!" With life and death situations you have to learn how to get that into your head fast, or else you won't last long. If you're training in the dojo you might be thinking about "how many points do I need to win this match", or "I know he uses a round house kick a lot after he throws a straight punch, so I need to…", very rarely is it "You're going down!"

Think back to your most recent sparring match. What were you thinking about? What thoughts ran through your head – consider the brief blips of thought as well? Write down those thoughts. What are they? Are they powerful messages of victory? Or decaying darts of doubt, fear, anger and negativity?

The core thought of a mindset of surviving and triumphing is the phrase "I will win!" Once you get that into your head that you will never lose, you won't – now it's not simply saying to yourself "I'm going to win this" and shrug it off casually, but it takes some special training and some deep ingraining.

Imagine the perfect training routine. What does it consist of? Are there special mindset drills? Are there physical drills that back up those thoughts? They both need to be there if you want progress, real progress. Over the years I used a variety of techniques over and over to develop my mind set (Physical and

Mental Exercises). In fact I didn't fully recognize it until years later. I had been drilling my subconscious mind that whenever I am in a fight I win, no matter what. I've refined these techniques and expanded on them and seen a drastic change in how my students spar and act in the Dojo – they truly are remarkable and you will not think the same after you have used them.

Imagine the mind of a *Fighting Genius* – that is what you will become. These training methods are life changing and you're in luck because you're going to learn them here! We'll cover more on the subject of mindset in detail in Chapter Six.

There are so many aspects we can analyze and pick apart with this type of scenario, and we will cover other principles that will directly affect the street fighting situation in later chapters. The *Ideas* behind Street Fighting have been around for quite some time, and in some ways is more "natural" or an animalistic way of fighting than the traditional Eastern Martial Arts. Those concepts fit closely to human nature, and when one is able to identify, apply in a controlled fashion and use those concepts, that person is far more deadly than your average black belt.

A Darker Side to Things

Outside of Street Fighting there are other aspects to consider in this World. A man who had a unique life, who once practiced traditional styles, was in the military and hit rock bottom and eventually ended up in jail and later cleaned himself up, shared a very unique observation on the subject of this "real world of fighting". He had not been in many fights of his own, before the military, and after some time in the service he saw matured martial artists losing in brutal matches to average men who only had street experience, and minimal combat training – why? Part of it goes back to the principles we talked about before, others we will discuss later on. He then explained his experience in jail, and that there in jail he found some very sick monsters who indulged in the subject of killing. Their purpose was discovering and finding new ways to tear their next victim apart with their bare hands. Imagine fighting someone like that. They would be deadly opponents. They would have the ability to strike fear and terror into the hearts and minds of all their victims. Wouldn't you call that a *Monster*?

The idea of an ever evolving monster is a very accurate picture of what the real world is like – that is not to say every person who fights on the street is a monster, but that new strategies are invented and discovered all the time. This life is about evolving, perfecting what we have done before and finding new ways of accomplishing the task at hand. Therefore as we continue to grow and practice in the Martial Arts we too must evolve our methods and strategies in dealing with real world encounters, something we will cover in greater detail in Chapter Five. But for now keep that on your mind, and do this exercise.

EXERCISE

Grab a piece of paper and write the phrase "My Martial Arts skills are always growing and adapting to any situation" – note how you feel about this phrase.
- Now that it is written down repeat it out loud to yourself ten times.
- Next use your less dominate eye to read it ten times (you find your less dominate eye by focusing on an object in front of you with both eyes opened, then close each eye alternating which one is opened. The eye with the shifted image is your less dominate eye).

- And finally, take a pencil and write with your less dominate hand the phrase ten times.

Now that you're done, do you see the difference? Does this phrase resonate with you a little more than it did when you first read it? It feels slightly more real than it did before, right? This is what we call an ALT, Accelerated Learning Technique, by doing this exercise you penetrate this phrase more deeply in your mind than you would by just reading it, or memorizing it. Now it is a part of you, and when you do this type of exercise over and over for this and other phrases you'll start to see a drastic change in your abilities, I guarantee it.

The Principle of *continual adaptation* and growth has been around for centuries, and I would say it is part of every person's being to have a desire to grow and progress. Our 'styles' shouldn't become dead after we have reached a goal, achieved a rank, won a tournament, etc, but rather continued to be worked on and perfected. In order for you to become the 'Ultimate Warrior', you have to continually progress.

Now that we've covered some things about the real world, what it's like and what we can do to counter it, let's go deeper. Let's examine some profound principles that I and other Great Martial Artists have discovered, and show you some ways of implementing them in your life. Are you ready? Let's go!

Chapter Two
Philosophies

"To unlearn is the highest achievement man can obtain."

What is a Martial Philosophy? Philosophies are the guidelines of styles. They're the rules, the do's and do not's. They govern the mind of the Martial Artist not only in combat but in everyday life. Philosophies are what make styles different. Think about it, a Side Kick is always a Side Kick, the mechanics are the same, but the ways of implementing it are different – that's Philosophy.

In this chapter we will outline and discuss key principles and philosophies that will *revolutionize* the way you fight, spar, and train.

End a fight quick!

Often in real life situations things are not drug out ordeals. They happen fast, and they end fast – and if you don't end it fast your opponent will. The Great Sun Tzu said…

> "In War, Victory should be *swift*. If victory is slow men tire, morale sags, sieges exhaust strength; protracted campaigns strain the public treasury… I have heard that in war haste can be folly but never seen delay that was wise."
>
> - Sun Tzu (Minford, 2002)

Let's break apart the meaning of this phrase– we can look at war as realistic combat, Sun Tzu gives clearly the reasons why in war you don't want to drag things out. Plainly put you use up your resources. In a fight or match we have resources too, mainly our energy, focus, and strategy. If we drag it out and make it flashy, show off, etc, we in turn tire, if things look bad we might get worried thus affecting our mindset, our strikes won't have real power behind them, we endanger ourselves, we anger our opponent, the list could go on and on – to sum it up it's bad to drag it out.

In order for us to end a fight quickly we need a couple of things; speed, agility, power, firm wits, and iron determination.

Speed - What is the definition of speed? Distance over Time, or the time it takes to cover a certain distance.

So how do you make sure you are faster than the other guy? Well the simple answer is training; the better answer is proper training. There is a difference between speed and power; it's about how fast your arm moves not how much it can move. We'll talk about developing speed in Chapter Three.

Agility - Are you as light as a feather? The Trick to agility is footwork, footwork, footwork. If you want to be more agile than the competition you need to train hours on footwork. Correct footwork will end a fight faster than anything else. I have some footwork exercises for you in Chapter Three.

Power - Take a moment and picture in your mind the most powerful thing you know of. What is it? Now take a moment and jot down everything about it that makes it powerful. The things you see will be completely unique. There is no right or wrong answer. Here's an example from myself of just one thing.

When I think of power I'm taken back to my childhood to a TV series called *Tranzor Z*, to me that robot was the pinnacle of power;

- It was *huge*.

- It could *take out anything*.
- It fought for truth and right.
- A *defender* of peace.
- Nothing stood in its way.
- And it was almost *indestructible*.

The things I connected with power from this TV series stuck with me and they were the basis of some of my mindset practices for years.

Now how can you adopt those things? Perhaps you already have – hats off to you! Certain thoughts will come to your mind of things you can do, write them down and DO THEM! Keep these notes you'll need them for a later exercise. Keep expanding your list. If there are multiple things that come to your mind, write all of them down. List every point about power for each thing. This is an unlimited exercise.

Firm wits - What are Firm wits?
- You got to keep your head cool, the longer you drag out the fight the faster your head "warms up".
- You also have to learn to manage controlling your body's urge to use adrenaline. This is something not too many people understand, but in a fight you don't want your adrenaline to kick in, that's a last ditch effort – also it is well known in the medical field that when your body uses adrenaline your body tires quicker. If you recognize that rush, you better end it quick. In order to control your

adrenaline you need to control your emotions. You control your emotions by your mindset and how you look at objects and situations.

Iron Determination - This is all about your mental programming. Iron Determination comes from long and nurturing positive reinforcement, both mentally and physically. You have to truly belief, not just with your conscious mind but your subconscious mind. You must have absolutely no doubt, "one percent doubt and you're out".

Let's look at something from history that backs up these things. Imagine Feudal Japan, an almost empty street and two traditionally dressed Samurais. Both of them are standing in a position, ready to draw their swords. When the Samurai would be challenged on the street the fight wasn't a flashy display of skill and swordsmanship. Rather it would end soon after they drew their swords. It was about who would *strike* who *first* and *end* it. Visualize the faces on those men, the speed their arms move to cut through their opponent. That is what you must become. So next time you get corned in an alley, or you're on the mat practicing, remember the Samurai.

You need an "Offensive Defense"

This is a term that comes from Bruce Lee, in his various books, interviews and statements he talks about this "Offensive Defense" and that it is the key to any victory. Essentially the whole principle behind this philosophy is attack as they attack. Use their momentum against them. When they are coming at you and you hit, there is a greater amount of force behind it. No one expects a punch or a kick to hit them while they're attacking you; rather they expect a defensive move.

In order to really internalize this you have to be thinking "When they come at me, I come at them even harder." "I do not step back when I am attacked, I step forward." This way of thinking and acting is so unconventional to most fighters, and it can really throw your opponent for a loop!

The principle of offensive defense is one that needs to be constantly pushed. It's a proactive approach to fighting, it's not a he hits, I block, I hit, he blocks type of thing. It's a disruptive pattern. When you have an offensive defense you're the one in control, you are the orchestrator of the fight.

Let me give you an example from my life. Before I studied Jeet Kune Do I mainly used techniques from Karate and Wing Chun and was guided by the philosophies of both schools. I had various sparring partners, most if not all were black belts, from styles of Tae Kwan Do, Karate, and Kung Fu. I did all right in the matches, it was pretty even. I was disciplined and methodical with my Katas and combinations. In some ways I was predictable. After discovering Jeet Kune Do, and more especially this concept of offensive defense, my sparring matches completely changed. In fact it was so stunning to my sparring partners that they were perplexed with my new way of fighting, and I hardly ever lost a sparring match from that point on. This combined with "Broken Rhythm", something we'll explain more in this chapter, were the two most powerful principles that changed my way of fighting forever!

- Speed is a critical factor in effectively using this "Offensive Defense".

- You have to move faster than your opponent moves.
- Your reaction time has to be faster than your opponent.
- When he punches or kicks, you need to hit by the time he's half way through with the strike.

Now that takes some talent, in fact only a fraction of the Martial Artist out there will be able to do this. You might have some doubts if you're in that small percentage, so I'm going to help you out and teach you a few things that can tip that average in your favor.

EXERCISE

Number 1: Make your mind believe you're fast enough. Here are a couple of things we can do to get you "up to speed" in your mind.
Write the phrase down "I am FASTER than ANY of my opponents" – now the key words are FASTER and ANY, those are the things you want your mind to believe. You are the fastest fighter in the world! No one can match your speed! Now go and practice some punches, and while you're punching keep repeating in your mind that phrase "I am FASTER than ANY of my opponents", if you want to go the extra mile, repeat in your mind phrases that are like that one. Just keep the phrase up front in your mind as your punching, I'll explain why later. You can also do the exercise we did earlier in Chapter One with your less dominate hand and eye to enhance this exercise.

Number 2: Use weights. In order to physically get faster you need to use extra weight. You need to weigh yourself down, so your body gets used to moving in a restricted environment.

Go running with weighted cloths and work up your 1 mile or 2 mile or 4 mile run to what it was before you had the weights (now that's really a killer, not only do you get a faster run but your footwork is greatly affected).

Punch and Kick with weights. Use either dumbbells or weighted wrist/ankle bands. As your progress add more and more weight. Start with something small, five pounds each and work up to twenty and more.

Another exercise is a more of a life style change, and you'll have to get used to it, but it's definitely worth it! Here's a story.

When I started my intensive training I would wear weights throughout the whole day! I only took them off to sleep and shower. Because I weighed myself down I saw a tremendous change in my non weighed environment. Everything felt lighter; I could move faster, moving at the rate my mind and body thought was normal.

You get so used to the extra weight that when you take it off your mind is so accustomed to the weights that it sends signals to move with the same amount of force (thus increasing your speed because there is less resistance). Imagine, you go to grab a glass and you grab it like lightening, and with hardly any effort. It also seems that by doing this, reaction time speeds up. Perhaps it is because the mind is used to limbs being heavier that it has to process movement faster than it would without the weight. Now this might not be practical for everyone, certain work environments might not appreciate you walking around with weights on your arms and legs (though the legs can be easily covered with pants). So adapt this as much as you can, and start out light, don't hurt yourself, ok?

Stealth in your actions is critical for victory

If your opponent doesn't know what's coming next they will have a pretty hard time defending against you. Deception is a great tool to employ in hand to hand combat, in fact the Great Sun Tzu described the art of Deception as…

> "The Way of War is A Way of Deception. When able feign inability… when near, appear far; when far appear near. Lure with bait; strike with chaos"
>
> - Sun Tzu (Minford, 2002)

Deception can come in various forms and vary from situation to situation. In order to win on the battlefield you must become a Master of Deception.

During my early days of martial arts I would always get into a stance to start a match or to defend myself in a street fight, and just stand there in the stance. As I grew in the arts I tried out new tactics, tested some theories and I found that deception can easily tip the scales in any battle.

Here are some things I found helpful in my discovery and application of Deception.

Number 1: Shizen No Kamae – In Ninjutsu the starting stance for anything is this Shizen No Kamae, or as translated into English, the natural stance. Everything flows from this stance even the traditional "ready stance" we learn in our traditional martial arts training.

Here's an experience from Anshu Steven Hayes, "…'Please throw a punch at Tanemura-san.'

The master's assistant rose to his feet and moved close to me. He appeared to be in his late twenties and, though not as tall as I, was of solid build. I hesitated for a moment, not knowing how to handle the situation. The man stood there in a relaxed manner. What should I do? Should I really try to hit him? I waited for him to get ready. 'Please. Throw a punch at Tanemura-san.' He was just standing there when I finally let loose a right-hand punch that ripped through the air toward his face.

He moved as effortlessly as a curtain in the wind to the inside of my punch, letting my fist sail through the empty space where his face had been. Flipping his left fist up and across, he struck my punching hand beneath the thumb. It was over in half a second. He had punched my punch and my whole arm felt as though it had turned to ice. The tingling, frozen feeling extended from armpit to fingertips; my hand hung limp, incapable of opening. I must have looked absolutely pitiful, for both men laughed and shook their heads." (Hayes, 1981). Think about it, not many martial artists start out a match just standing there, I mean wouldn't you think the guy is not all there? You might even have a boost of your own ego experiencing this first hand (and therein lies some of the deception).

I can also tell you from my own experience this really throws people for a loop! Some of my more traditional sparring partners were a tad bit frustrated at my "attempts to mock them" (and it wasn't out of a desire to spite them, it was something practical I had learned and I was simply sharing it). Needless to say all of those matches started the same way – a startled reaction, which eventually lead to my opponent losing the match.

So let's break down the Shizen No Kamae. WHY this tactic is so effective.

- **Your attacks can't be predicted.** When you're standing normally with your hands at your side, your back straight, and your neck relaxed your opponent can't read where something is coming from. It's a complete tossup. Is there going to be a kick, a punch, what?! Not only do you get a surprise attack, but it mentally throws off your opponent, especially if you're in a traditional match. In most cases you both start out with a bow and transition into some kind of stance, you're both mentally ready to strike each other. But when you're standing there normally and your opponent is in their stance it's not quite clicked in their brain that they're in a match. The longer you stand there the more they take themselves out of the match, and as they do that's your time to strike. If you do it right you'll always land the first hit, no matter how fast their reflexes are or the amount of their skill. You will make contact and when you do the match is over, they've lost, you've got the upper ground, you're free to unleash your fury – and all the while, even though you're not in a traditional stance, you're so in the match.

- **It doesn't make sense to your opponent**. Like we said the mental connection isn't there or it's starting to weaken. Sometimes you'll perplex your opponent, especially if you've not fought them before. They'll start to back down, or if they don't they'll attack with some restraint – but it will never be to the full potential as it would have been if you were in your traditional on-guard stance. This reaction will sometimes cause your opponent to lose confidence, which gives you another foothold in the fight or the match.
- **It's just all out weird to some people.** They just don't comprehend why you're doing it. It causes them to stop and think, which is your opportunity to strike. Remember this is all about deception, you're tricking them into thinking you're not fighting, and you're just standing there, right? But on the contrary you're poised for your attack, you're more ready than ever, as Sun Tzu said, "When near appear far… lure with bait; strike with chaos." (Minford, 2002) Surely this principle allows you to do all that. By standing there you appear far, you lure them with the bait of peace or a truce, and then you Strike with Chaos and Fury! For the average person this is a process not

understood or grasped, but now you know it, and when you use it you'll be a master of deception!

Number 2: Feigns. Feigning is one of the greatest tools in combat. By feigning a strike you can create an opening, and ultimately end the match or the fight. Most schools teach about feigning so I won't delve too deep into it, if you want to learn more you can take one of our classes and become a part of our Academy. A combination of feigns and actual strikes will greatly increase your odds in a fight. And to take it even further, a double, triple of quadruple strikes works wonders, they in themselves are feigns, mainly because only one strike is meant to hit.

Feigning in a fight can really trip up your opponent, especially when the feign and the actually strike are coming from two different directions. When you're seeing a punch come at you, you're not too concerned about the legs beneath, nor do you see them come at you because you're too preoccupied with the punch.

The secret to feigning is speed, and your ability to weave it seamlessly into your movements. To make fake appear real, and real to appear fake. You must cover your true intentions with your fake ones; distract the eyes of your opponent as far away as possible from where you intend to strike.

EXERCISE

If you can, go grab a sparring partner, if not try when you have a sparring match – now strike at their face with a feign, pull it back about 1 to 3 inches from their face, and as you're striking come up with a kick to the leg or stomach (don't feign that one). Discuss it with them and see what they thought – did they see the kick? What were they focusing on?

Now that you see the power of feigning use it! Practice with it; get good at pulling your punches just inches away from the target to make it appear real.

Number 3: Body Language. By simply turning your head and looking around gives off signals of "I'm not comfortable", "what's gonna happen". There are other signals you can give off to loosen up your opponent. Darting you eyes around, the position of your shoulders, how straight or not straight your back is. When not controlled these are all signs of fear, lack of confidence, low self esteem and weakness. But when controlled are powerful allies. When you control your body language you control what you're opponent thinks.

As you do these motions reactions in your opponent's mind bubble up in the form of "oh this will be easy", "what a push over", "I thought this guy was tougher than that". They start to loosen up, and they become lax in their attitude toward the fight. Their mind is handing over the victory to you, if you're in control. Just by doing this you've broken down some of the mental structures your opponent needs to win the fight, and thereby you weaken them without lifting a finger.

Once you can control your body language and use it to lure in your opponent and trap them you'll triumph over anyone not ready to expect deception.

*** Warning *** Do not let these simple movements take over your ability to win. If you're not in control with the intent to deceive you can even trick yourself into thinking you're not strong enough or bold enough to take on your opponent. At all times you must have the intent of victory and survival foremost in your mind while doing any of these movements!

Now some of you might say "Deception isn't honorable" or "I have a code of honor, I can't trick someone" or "Good people don't use deception". Well integrity is a great virtue to posses, but not in a fight. It's all about to conquer or to be conquered. Those are the only two options, and those who cling to their honor in a fight sometimes don't come out the victor – and on the street you'll end up dead.

Mindset is more important than skill and strength

Have you ever seen a match and saw the two opponents and knew for sure that a certain one would win? I was watching a boxing match one time and I leaned over to my wife at the beginning of the match and said "He's gonna win" and my wife responded "how do you know, the other guys is undefeated". My response was, "the look in his eyes, he's already won the match I can see it, it's definitely lacking in the other guy", by round ten of the twelve round match the man I said would win won, and his opponent was bloodied and black and blue.

So what was in this guy's eyes that made his victory so apparent? Was it arrogance? Was it self-pride? Perhaps it was a little bit of both, but what he had was true determination to conquer, he knew in his mind he was going to win and that he was going to take the other guy out! His mindset was in the right place.

Expect Deception

Deception is the antithesis to a healthy mindset; Deception can break down the strongest fighters, if their minds are weak. In order to have the mindset to win you must always be aware that the other person could be deceiving you with a feigned weakness or some other sort of trickery. Never rule out that someone would deceive you in a fight, there is always a trap. The real question is what is it?

"Broken Rhythm"

Bruce Lee enlightened the world with his philosophy into life and martial arts. The concept of broken rhythm was almost unheard of before his time. Broken Rhythm is flexibility, the ability to weave in and out of patterns. To see broken rhythm in action all one needs to do is observe water. Water flows through cracks, pools in beds, and opens and erodes new gateways for new water to flow through.

To posses Broken Rhythm is to be able to weave in and out of styles, both of your own and that of your opponent. You spot or create the opening and you attack with the precise tool to get the job done, there and then. Your combinations shift and change with the reaction and movement of your opponent. There is no same combination, they might be similar, but each plays to the unique tune of that battle, and no two battles are the same.

One thing I've noticed is that when someone from a strict style is fighting or sparring with someone who knows and has become the principle of Broken Rhythm, the one with the strict style always gets frustrated. They always get interrupted by the other person. Broken

Rhythm is the antithesis of Katas, it is that 'water' that erodes away at strict fighting styles, creating new gateways for you to enter and triumph.

Here are some key aspects for developing Broken Rhythm

- Forget what you've learned. Don't allow previous combinations and instruction to be the only things that guide your movements.
- Just Act, don't think. Let you subconscious mind do all the work, it will calculate strategy faster than you can.
- Keep your mind clear. This goes along with the previous point, if your mind is clear your body is free to move and express itself in a manner that will be the most efficient, precise and powerful.
- Focus on the here and now. If your mind is wondering "what's going to happen next?" you've lost, and while you're figuring things out in your head you're getting the crap beat out of you.
- Sparring. In your sparring practice have your partner perform certain combinations and identify the holes. Observe and record which punch or kick would be the most effective in stopping your opponent.

One way you can look at broken rhythm is to envision a professional piano player, playing a grand piece of music, perhaps Mozart's Requiem. All of a sudden a child appears and begins to bang on the piano, catching the pianist off guard, startling him. The sounds become noisy and grotesque. The beautiful melody has become blurred with the tones of unevenness, lack of methodical precision and disturbing sounds. In a way, most of your opponents might be like this professional pianist, their movements are beautiful and timed perfectly, resulting in a beautiful display of technique and form, but like the pianist when the 'unlearned' appears and begins to interfere, the beauty becomes ugliness, the precision marred. In a concert this is unacceptable, but in a fight the unlearned or those who have undone their way of learning will always destroy the beauty of traditional styles. And this is perfectly acceptable.

Broken Rhythm isn't to be sloppy. It's to have even more precision than your opponent, to have quicker reflexes, and greater presence of mind than your opponent. Broken Rhythm is a process of unlearning what you've conditioned yourself with over the years. This combined with the principle of Offensive Defense greatly changed the way I fought in sparring matches, tournaments and on the street. These two principles alone will completely change your fighting style.

Broken Rhythm is not just a philosophy but a life style change; it's a governing principle that drastically changes the course of one's development in the martial arts.

The Voice is often mightier than the Fist

One determining factor in a fight is the use of one's voice. Now you might not think your voice has much power or even any power at all, but in this section we'll discuss how powerful your voice can be.

The Japanese understood the principle that words can change the world around you. "Kotodama", the spirit of words as translated into English are words that have spiritual power behind them. In many of the world's religions there are special words that have certain spiritual significance or power when said. The concept that words have power behind them is nothing new. The practice of using these words has been around for thousands of years. The Egyptians used "Key words" in certain ceremonial rites, and believed they were essential to one's eternal journey.

Not just in religion, but also in Martial Arts the principle of Spiritual Words shows up pretty frequently. Aikido is one particular style of martial art that is focused on these spiritual words. The words of an Aikido practitioner are extremely powerful, and if you've ever seen one in action you can tell that they're exerting very little physical energy to do what they do. Well how do they do it? It's these special words, words also known as a Kiap, or Kiai.

Religion and Martial Arts aren't the only areas you see this. Mainly a cultural distinction, many Japanese animation TV series and movies have this concept of key words; more especially the Martial Arts based anime series (but it appears in others genres as well). More often than not you'll hear a command before a character uses a technique or sometimes before entering a battle. These scenes can be silly at times but the principle behind them is very profound. You might not shout in a battle "Gravity Punch!" but you can still project power in other ways that are equally effective and not so ridiculous.

Kiap (or Kiai): to kiap is to use your voice together with your movement, your strike, your grapple, or your submission and your spirit. A Kiap is a projection of your intended movement physically, mentally, emotionally and spiritually. Not only does your strike hit and go through your opponent but so does your voice or the energy behind it. Your voice is a "sonic strike". It has a very strong mental impression upon your opponent, and in some cases will startle them enough to stop them dead in their tracks.

For instance, many schools that teach self defense will use a command or a "HA!" sound in combination with their punch or kick. If you're learning how to stop an opponent you might shout in your kiap "Stop it!" in combination with your block or parry. If you're knocking someone to the ground you might use "Get down!" The words themselves are powerful, because the other person's subconscious mind will pick up on it and do it, especially when there is a commanding presence behind the words – it happens almost without their recognition.

Let's look at two situations. Two black belts are practicing. Both were taught by the same instructor, both trained similar amounts of hours, both are in similar physical condition. For their first sparring match they don't use any kiaps. The fight is pretty even. The next round one of them uses Kiaps with their techniques and there is a dramatic change in the outcome of the match. The one who did not use kiaps had less power behind his punches and kicks, backed down slightly when the black belt who Kiaped was on the offense. The one who used Kiaps was mostly on offense while the other was playing the defense most of the time.

When one uses a Kiap it gives an overpowering presence, and in a way, on a primal level, shows you are the dominate one. Kiaping uses your vocal cords in a specific way to project your mindset onto the other person, or persons. Your voice is 'more full' during a kiap, which gives it the dominating presence.

Here are a couple of things we should look at when learning how to do and use a kiap:

Number 1: Mindset. When learning and applying a kiap, mindset is the first step. You need to get it into your head what it's for, where you do it, and why you do it. We're going to do an exercise so get ready.

EXERCISE
Take a piece of paper and right down the phrase "My Kiap is meant to overpower others", and repeat it out loud ten times. Write it with your less dominate hand ten times, and read it with your less dominate eye ten times. Repeat this exercise with the following phrases "My voice is full and powerful when I kiap." "I am ferocious when I Kiap!" "I use my kiap in any martial situation" "I kiap to win and protect myself" "I kiap because I am the ultimate warrior!"

Ok so now that you've got this stamped into your head let's actually do a Kiap.

Number 2: Practice! Ok now go find a place where you're not going to startle anyone, or maybe you feel embarrassed about "yelling" and you don't want to practice around people. Either way, find a quite place. Throw a punch and shout 'Ha!" – was it whimpy? Was it too much yelling? Did it seem scattered? Try it again and focus your voice on where you're punching. It's going to take some creativity – imagine a target in front of you and hit it with your fist and your voice. How did that feel? How was it different? Keep focusing on one point and practice over and over.

Number 3: Practical application. This is one of the most important steps to making a Kiap a part of you. Practical Application will solidify your mindset to your strikes.

EXERCISE

Find someone you trust maybe a fellow sparring partner, friend or family member and practice your punch and kiap combo – you might want them to hold a shield or a really huge pillow. Take some notes when doing this and have them observe the difference. First, punch normally with no kiap. Then the second time with a kiap. What was the difference? How did they feel each time? How did you feel each time?

Now you have a simple process, I suggest using this with every technique you've learned, it'll drastically change how you fight in a match or on the street.

Since we have finished that training exercise, let's take a look at what it's like in the real world. When you're out on the street, and in a confrontation most likely the other person will be acting tough trying to pin you down, either trying to taking your money, put you into submission, steal something, try to prove something, get back at you, whatever the reason, they want to be the superior one. A kiap can make a huge difference with the outcome of the fight. Your voice can easily shift the balance of dominance between you and your opponent, and you don't even have to throw a punch. Just by speaking with a full, over powering tone can stop the fight, and ideally that's the desired outcome, we don't want to be jumping into a fight if it's avoidable. Sun Tzu advised…

MARTIAL ARTS: Ultimate Warrior   Chapter Two

> "Ultimate excellence lies not in winning every battle but in defeating the enemy without ever fighting."
>
> - Sun Tzu (Minford. 2002)

Every situation is different so we can't give one straight solution for using your voice. The key is to keep a cool head and use a kiap like tone. If that doesn't work I guess you might have to put the other guy in submission or out of commission.

If things do turn south, and you end up in a fight, it can be ended quickly using kiaps. The attacker won't be used to a ferocious 'victim', which will take them off guard, thus creating an opening for you to launch a counter offensive. Using command phrases with your strikes will greatly affect the outcome. For instance what is the desired outcome of the fight? Is it to pin the guy down and wait for the police? Cause him to run way? Leave him shivering in his boots? Whatever it may be you need to play every strike and kiap to that end.

Here's an activity for you. Visualize a situation. Create the attacker and all their actions. Write out all the strikes and kiaps, then role-play it with a sparring partner. Keep doing it and creating new ideas and ways to deal with various situations.

Using your voice to trigger mental imagines and control your opponent is another technique outside of Kiap that can work wonders, especially on the weak minded. No these are not "Jedi Mind Tricks", this is more along the lines of hypnosis. If you're using an over powering tone of voice, like with a kiap you can inflict a lot of doubt into your opponent. That's the underlying principle here, your _tone of voice_, after that the remaining variables are the commands or the impressions you want to impress on your opponents mind. (Note these principles tie in deeply with your own mindset; they HAVE to be deeply ingrained into you first in order for them to work.)

The whole point of this principle is to get across to your opponent that you're in command, you're the strongest here, and you won't lose – they're the one who is going to lose. In a way this is a type of brainwashing – let's call it In Combat Brainwashing.

First let's define Brainwashing:

> **Brainwashing:** The act of cleaning out or erasing past or previous mental beliefs and replacing them with new ones.

For instance, in this book we do a type of brainwashing to help you improve yourself and become the ultimate warrior. There is brainwashing in everything; it's a part of our society, our marketing, our advertising, our upbringing by our parents. All of these are a type of brainwashing. Let's clear this up – brainwashing is not bad. It's what people do with it that makes it good or bad. Another term for brainwashing is mental-linking, or to be more scientific it's the rewiring of synapses in our brain.

Now that we have defined brainwashing here are the basic steps to develop In-Combat Brainwashing.

Number 1: Start with yourself. You need to deeply belief that you're the one, you're the top dog, and no one can beat you (refer to "Mindset" earlier in this Chapter and Chapter Six for more details). You truly belief with every fiber of your being that you are the best and you can adapt and grow to have that outcome in every situation. Your mind and body can and will do remarkable things when you have this mindset. A great way to do this is to visualize yourself winning all the time. Then to solidify this, experience winning situations often in your life, in the real world, in training and in your mind (we'll cover mental sparring in Chapter Seven). These situations don't have to be solely based on Martial Arts, it can be anything from finishing a book, completing a training program, finishing your homework, completing a task at work – the list can go on forever!

Number 2: Everything you are, is opposite in your opponent. If you're the best, they're the worst, if you're the strongest, they are the weakest. The principle of opposition or duality plays the major role in setting this up. What are you? Then whatever you are, your opponent is the opposite. Internalize this, you must believe it, you do believe, I believe it. Master this underlying principle and you'll be able to take out anyone.

Number 3: Develop the phrases for your opponent. Here you put into action the principle of opposition, you write down everything they are, and you visualize in your head that it is THEM not you that fit these descriptions. Always whenever you say, read, write or hear these words they apply to your opponent never you! NEVER YOU! Never to me. By doing this it secures you mindset and strengthens it as you practice and encounter these sayings in real life.

Number 4: Use them in your practice. As you train, either on a bag, or in a shadow sparring match (we'll cover more on that in Chapter Eight) visualize your opponent and project the thought onto them. Start out in your mind and build it up to when you really believe it say it out loud in your training.

Number 5: Mingle in positive phrases for yourself, with the negative for them. By doing this you build a gap, you are ever going up and they are ever going down (all this in their minds), a gap they can never cross, you will always be light years ahead of them. For instance "I will be victorious, you will never beat me!"

> "These Five point the way to Victory. Hence the saying 'Know the enemy, know yourself, and victory is never in doubt, not in a hundred battles.' He who knows self but not the enemy will suffer one defeat for every victory, he who knows neither self nor enemy will fail in every battle."
>
> - Sun Tzu (Minford, 2002)

By applying these things, in an abstract way, you know your enemy and yourself before the battle starts. (Note the five steps for in-combat brainwashing were not taken from the teachings of Master Tzu.)

Not only should you use phrases, but questions. Questions trigger the subconscious mind, if you supply the question and the answer; they then get two answers. This will result in confusion – and perhaps eventually cause them to believe what you're saying. For instance ask "Who is the victor... I AM!" "Who is the strongest? I AM you are the

WEAKEST!" Questioning your opponent will cause doubt and confusion that you can use to your advantage in a fight. Also putting an emphasis on the words you wish you get across the most will cause a deeper impact on your opponent's mind. There is no limit to these types of questions. Your imagination is your only limitation. You further emphasis and anchor the knowledge of yourself and your enemy by using questions. I've always won by a landslide whenever doing this; it's definitely a killer way of fighting!

A Fit novice is better than an out of shape master

Fitness sometimes is a matter over looked by some martial artists. Imagine a car. When you don't do regular maintenance, fill up with the right gasoline, air up the tires, service the engine, rotate the tires, by new tires, we could go on with this but we won't – will your car run as well as the guy who owns the same model and maintains it daily? Of course not! So why not maintain our bodies?

When I came on the scene to the martial arts, physical fitness was never discussed. In fact it took me almost nine years to finally realize and appreciate the power of this principle. I always thought "technique is everything. If I got the right techniques nothing can happen to me" Needless to say during the time I thought this I was pretty out of shape; I was around 5'8" and about 220 pounds. And yes you get another story; you're going to like this one.

Now during my early years as a martial artist I worked out, build some muscle, had some strength, lifted weights and what not, but I wasn't in shape, I still was carrying around a lot of fat. I never did any true conditioning. Up until the time I discovered Bruce Lee's Jeet Kune Do I was in mediocre shape. After only a month and a half of Bruce's Training Program I was down to 150 pounds, and about 8% body fat, and before my year mark I was 155 pounds and 5% body fat. Some other details, I went from a 36 inch waist to a 28 inch waist, my max weight lifting weight before was now my toning weight, my mile time went from a staggering 10 min mile to a 4:48 min mile. On the martial arts side, I was able to do continuous sparring matches, heavy contact for over an hour straight, no breaks! During that time and after I didn't lose a single sparring match, or street fight, period!

This story illustrates a point, physical fitness does matter! I saw a drastic change in my life and you will too when you start to implement this philosophy. Here are the key areas in implementing physical fitness into your Martial Arts Regimen;

- Diet.
- Supplements.
- Flexibility.
- Strength Training.
- Weight Training.
- Cardiovascular training.
- Technique Training (punches, kicks, etc. weighted and non-weighted).

All these areas improve your abilities and cause you to appear "super human" in the eyes of some. In this section we'll briefly touch on each subject (for a more complete breakdown refer to my book *Martial Arts: Extreme Fitness*)

Diet - This is the foundational building block for ANY physical fitness program! Without the proper fuel you're not going to be able to fully apply this principle of physical fitness. I stuck with a basic pattern of eating; in fact I look at food solely for fuel, nothing else, not for pleasure, not for relaxation, fuel and fuel only. That was the FIRST step in getting my diet right. I know it's a tough step but you can do it, if I, a fat kid at the time could do it so can you.

After I understood this I began to choose a diet system that would best fit that. I needed to clean my body out, and changing my diet accomplished that.

- Rice and other like grains are the foundation of every meal.
- Accompanied with lean meats (such as lean beef with very low fat percentages, chicken, fresh fish – salmon [preferably Wild Alaskan], halibut, yellowtail, eel, octopus to name a few.).
- My Early and mid meals contained mostly fruits.
- My mid and evening meals contained vegetables.
- Occasionally I'd throw pasta into the mix, but not often.
- I cut out most sodium based flavoring and replaced them with spices and herbs.

Another big shift for me was my drinking habits (no I wasn't an alcoholic; I just like certain sodas, and other drinks). I made the shift strictly to water and pure juices, preferably hand squeezed juice. I changed my choice of milk and found low fat or organic soy to be the better choices.

Supplements - There are a wide range of supplements that one can take. The Basic list consists of:
- Multivitamin with a wide range of vitamins, minerals and other health formulas.
- Soy Lecithin supplement (preferably in Granule form to mix in with a drink or certain meals.).
- Bee pollen.
- Omega 3 supplement with vitamin –e based tocotrinels.
- Rose hips.
- Inositol.
- Liquid Nitric Oxide.
- Occasional ginseng in a combined mixture of honey something Bruce Lee called "Royal Jelly". (Lee, Bruce Lee, The Art of Expressing the Human Body, 1997)
- A muscle repair formula.
- And an antioxidant combination formula.

From personal experience I've noticed significant improvement by taking each of these supplements, and have come to my own personal conclusion that these are essential for reaching new heights physically.

*** **DISCLAMER** *** I do not make any scientific claims that these dietary supplements, cure or treat any form of illness, chronic, terminal or otherwise.

Flexibility - I found the most effective way to gain flexibility was stretching. I followed a stretching program that gave me greater flexibility in every area within months. Essentially I followed a simple formula, 4 reps 20 to 30 second holds. Sometimes I needed assistance to hold a position, and that's fine, just don't overdo it. You don't want to rip any muscles!

Yoga is also a great way to improve and gain flexibility and balance. Doing any type of Yoga is a great way to start gaining flexibility. Yoga coupled with stationary stretching will definitely skyrocket you to a whole new level of Martial Arts. I dedicated anywhere from an hour to hour and a half each day to these types of exercises.

Let me tell you a story about how flexibility saved me in a match. I was in a match with a state champion wrestler, and he was a pretty big guy, 6'2" and over 200 pounds. This was after my Jeet Kune Do training so I was pretty slim and flexible. About 30 seconds into our match he got me into a submission hold on the ground. Because of my training I was able to slip out of it (it's not one you can easily get out of without lots of training), which caught him off guard. It was his signature finishing move after all. He tried other grapples but the same result. After a few more seconds he was on the ground, and the match was over.

Strength Training - This type of training involves various types of exercises from
- Weight lifting.

- Callisthenic exercises (a group of organized exercises performed without any weights, other than your own body weight).
- Isometric exercises (i.e. same distance exercises, the joints are at the same position or distance while the muscle is contracting).
- Isotonic exercises (i.e. same tension exercises, the tension remains the same in the muscle yet the joints are moving).
- And stress positions (stationary positions, similar to Isometric exercises).

About two hours a day is dedicated to these types of exercises. Strength training is meant to build *strength*, not muscle mass, so the result is a *slim* muscular body. There's a great advantage to that – you gain greater agility in your movements and speed in everything else.

Weight Training - When I talk about weight training it's all encompassing;
- It's strength training with weights.
- It's Power Pyramid.
- It's weighted punches and kicks.
- Weighted running.
- Anything you can do to physically to slow yourself down with resistance, preferably a weight of some sorts.

Like I mentioned earlier in the chapter, this type of training will speed up your reflexes, and among other things improve your strength and speed greatly.

Cardiovascular Training - Here are a few of the types of exercises I'd use to strengthen my lungs and heart.
- Running.
- Jogging.
- Cycling.
- Footwork exercises.
- Jump training.

One unconventional way of improving your lungs is to train with a snorkeler (for those of you who have asthma or any other type of lung or heart disorder contact your physician before you try this). An example of how to use this is to drill techniques or shadow spar with it for a certain period of time. For instance if you're training for a sports competition and you want to be able to last in a 5 minute round, train with it for 5 minutes straight. In a way this is like weight training for your lungs. This is a type of resistance exercise. Be careful with how you use it – if you're not careful you will pass out, so build your lungs up with it, try 30 seconds and go from there. Most average people can handle 30 seconds.

Technique Training - The amount of time you spend on your techniques has a huge impact on your abilities. I'd throw about 10,000 punches and 8,000 or so kicks, that's per hand or leg. I used a heavy bag for half of that, and the other half a division of weighted and non-weighted strikes. I'd also spend time drilling other techniques like grapples and ground game techniques. To build up my arms I would use something called a Power Pyramid, and for you weight lifters you know what that is. Essentially you'll do 20 reps of each weight going up and then back down, I mainly did this with my punches, but it can works for your kicks too if you wear weights and change the weight every 20 kicks. Over all I'd spend two hours or so with these types of exercises.

My whole physical fitness program is quite lengthy. It lasts anywhere from five and a half hours to six and a half hours, nonstop training, sometimes I'd break up the program and handle two groups at a time. It's really what works best for you.

Everything is a Weapon

Let me ask you something, how many weapons do you have on you right now? Is your answer none? Two? Four? Well there are a lot more than that, let's start off with seventeen. You're probably thinking "what the heck!" right? Let's look at things differently, and also define what a weapon is

> **Weapon:** Anything used to inflict harm upon another person(s).

Now take a look at yourself again, how many weapons are there, and what are they? Write it down. What's on the list? Have you ever thought about those being weapons? We'll talk about a couple and broaden your vision.

- **Your head.** Now you might think this is odd but, your head can be a weapon when you're in a tight spot, for instance if you're in a hold and can't use your arms or legs or shoulders or elbows you can use your head.
- **Your Teeth.** Now biting might not work in a sports setting but it definitely does in a real life situation. Most people won't expect a bite. It's just not in the world's way of thinking. It's 'too animalistic' which makes it a perfect weapon.
- **Your hips.** It might not be effective, but from time to time you might find an opportunity to use your hips to counter or redirect your opponent, especially if you're in a grapple.

So what qualifies as 'everything'? Well anything! The chair right next to you, the hanger in your closet, the mouse connected to your computer, a light bulb, your keys, the gardening tools in your garage (that's what the ninja used!) Anything can be a weapon. You just have to look at everything differently. If you have to use the salt on the table in the packet, your tooth pick, we can keep going but we won't, I think you get the picture.

Your environment is your arsenal weaponry; use everything to your advantage. The trash bin in the alley is a weapon if used right. You don't need to pick up your weapon to use it, just manipulate it in some way, or cause your opponent to use it in a way that hurts them.

EXERCISE
Grab your note book and write down everything in the room you're in that can be used as a weapon. Have you ever thought about those as weapons

before? If so good! Take this a step further. Tomorrow keep your note book with you all day, jot down everything you see throughout your day as a weapon. I promise you, you will be surprised at the list you create.

Becoming their worst nightmare

One of the great psychological weapons we have in our employ is the ability to use and manipulate the fear of others. Now this might sound like a monstrous thing to do, but in some ways you have to 'appear' to be a monster in their eyes. Though none of us are monster, sometimes we must take the appearance of one in order to win on the battlefield. We can refer back to an earlier section in this chapter that talked about "In-Combat Brainwashing". This is merely an extension of that. In order to do this correctly you have to understand your opponent, there isn't a simple 1, 2… formula for doing this, and it takes a lot of work and experience dealing with the human psyche.

There are two simple foundational principles that give a great base to build on.
- **The Correct mindset**. In a way you have to "detach yourself" and dive into the role.
- **Mastery of In-Combat Brainwashing.** Specific voice tones, and the boldness to carry out what needs to be done.

These provide a basis to accomplish the process of monstrosity. Essentially you're aim is to strike fear into your opponent, cause them to worry, be slightly paranoid, enough for them to lose focus. The objective is for you to shake their firmness. If they have a strong mindset, break it. If they have solid techniques make them sloppy. You are their worst nightmare, and you're here to end it! Now some opponents might not be so easily toppled with these types of mental games, but you can definitely chisel away at them. If nothing else you will have the correct mindset to win.

Three Steps to Perfection

There are three grand principles to truly applying and internalizing anything. Do it the natural way, learn how to do it the correct way, forget how to do it. These are the three phases of progression, and each is a separate height of learning and understanding.

- **First.** Doing it naturally or in an animalistic way is how anyone starts out in fighting, period! This is the basic level of interaction, there is no skill and no training involved. Just simple reaction to whatever happens. There are two ways we react, either to fight or flight. Or to put it in a different perspective; Offense and Defense. To us we punch like what we think a punch should be without having any formal training. The things we do on this level are part of the base programming we have in our mind, a rough draft or a sketch in other words.
- **Second.** The phase or level of learning is the intellectual way of doing. This encompasses training, intellectual development, the learning and application of principles and philosophy, the road to mastery in a style (i.e. working towards your black belt), understanding how techniques work and why they work, and a form of consciously doing techniques, training or anything else related. Sparring on a conscious level, in the form of thinking "he'll strike with a

straight punch and I'll parry, then…" or any other "mind chatter" is part of this second level of development. Often a fighter at this level has pauses in his Katas or matches. Sometimes there is rigidity between movements, because he or she is piecing the movements together with their conscious mind.

- **Third.** To forget, or unlearn is the highest degree of development. For instance let's take a look at our bodies. When we were learning to walk we had to think consciously how to do it, "ok I raise my right leg up and stand on my left, move my right leg forward, stand on it, raise my left…" think about the time it took you to read that sentence, does it take you that long to take two steps? Probably not. Our walking is on a subconscious level, we don't have to think how to walk, and if we did we'd take forever to get anywhere! To unlearn is to imbed something deep into your subconscious mind, deep enough that you never have to consciously think about it again!

This principle of 'unlearning' is the pinnacle to Martial Arts Mastery. You might have to start off by thinking slow when you're in the dojo, as you're learning techniques or sparring for the first time. But as you keep doing it over and over, it starts to become a part of you. Think about how long it takes you to think out a kata – now contrast that to how long it takes you to think out taking two steps compared to actually walking two steps or running two steps (on average it takes five seconds to think out walking two steps at normal speed, and to actually take those two steps less than 1 second). Think about that, if you could speed up your kata by five times, how fast would that be? Can you see it? Do you believe it? Well you should because it's possible and I'll show you how.

The Great Secret to achieve this third and final level of development is getting it deep into your subconscious mind. At our Academy we help people get to this step faster than most other schools because we implement certain training tactics. On average I see people learning twice as fast as they were when they weren't using these – I'm not talking one or two students I mean the whole student body is learning faster. It'll take me more than the time we have in this book to share everything with you, but let me give you some things you can do right now to speed up your progression.

> **Number 1:** Believe that you can learn as fast as possible. You have to truly believe it, or else you're not going to be open to the idea of learning fast. I'm not talking about reckless fast and not taking away anything but, really understanding and grasping the principles, quickly!

> **Number 2:** Seeing, learning and teaching – one of the best ways to anchor something you've already learned is to share it with someone else, it doesn't matter who, just share it. Teaching is the great learner. At our Academy we don't just teach you, you teach too. Work with a partner. Partners are great for learning new things quickly. Now you might be embarrassed but who cares, your partner probably feels the same way, so just toss out the embarrassment and get on with the training!

Number 3: Use Accelerated Learning Techniques. At the Academy we employ a wide range of techniques, from using Affirmations or declarations, self visualization, Hypnotherapy, VAKS (Visual, Audio, Kinetic and Spirit exercises), to name a few. These techniques alone played a huge role in speeding up the learning for our students, and I guarantee they will for you when you use them.

Number 4: Practice, Practice, Practice. When you add the three earlier principles to practice and drilling you've really created a solid foundation for learning, and now you have your mind working it right, your spirit working it right, and now your body. All three parts of your core essence working together, and boom it's like an explosion! You skyrocket in your ability and skill. Not to mention that by applying the earlier three principles when you do practice you will do it right the first time and you won't second guess yourself.

By using these four steps and others we've seen a rapid increase in our student's ability to learn, grasp, and hold on to the things they learn. I've used forms of these all throughout my life as a martial artist, but never together until recently, and it's been a joy to see others take pride and joy in the levels of success that they've been reaching.

Throughout your life you're going to reach this phase of development for different things. This is a lifelong process to go through, and as you move on to this level of progression for each technique or principle or philosophy, there will always be more to master. Life is about growth, and if we stop growing we begin to die. Now this is not to discourage you, it's a wonderful thing, we have the opportunity to grow, to master ourselves, and learn, adapt and become better and better each day. And as we keep growing it becomes easier and easier to keep up the habit, we tend to attract growth into our lives.

The purpose of your life is to grow, better yourself, seek all the knowledge you can and apply that knowledge always, to incorporate that knowledge into your very being, and thus you fill the measure of your creation and are eligible to reach your fullest potential.

Chapter Three
Fitness

"To bet 'Fit' one must train body, mind and soul."

MARTIAL ARTS: Ultimate Warrior — Chapter Three

The physical body is the foundation for our study of the Martial Arts. Everything we do physically is determined by our level of fitness. As we detailed principles of fitness in Chapter Two you probably got some good ideas right?

EXERCISE

Well take a moment and jot them down. Which of those exercises are you doing now? What haven't you been doing? What was something you've never thought of before?

Here's a challenge, take that list write the phrase at the top "I will do…"; Put it up by your mirror in the bathroom, or above your bed, somewhere where you can see it in the morning, and read each morning the list of thing you are going to do today. Not what *you're* going to do sometime in the future. Today, you're *doing* the list. You're taking that 2 mile run, you're eating the right food, you're drilling 200 straight punches today, and you're lifting those weights – whatever it is do *it*! When you have the urge to do it, go do it! Don't hesitant, yeah I know it's hard but so is everything else in life and you do that too, there is no difference in this list or anything else you do in life – it's all the same! The only reason you think it's hard is your mindset.

In this chapter we're going to talk about certain things we need to do as a martial artist, and I'll give you some tips to get it done. We'll also cover a light training program that anyone can implement into their lives. I will give you a basic diet program you can build and modify as you need to. I'll also go into detail of various products that can help you in your training. You are definitely going to be empowered!

Physical Requirements

Some of the basic things you need to have as a martial artist are these; *Flexibility* in your arms, legs, torso, wrists and ankles. There must be *Strength* behind your strikes and grapples. You need *Endurance* in your heart, lungs, and muscles. These are the three basic areas you *need* to focus on; everything else is an extension of one of these three areas.

Flexibility

Some Essential Flexibility exercises that you can do are static stretching, focusing on flexibility in these areas:
- Shoulders.
- Chest.
- Back.
- Legs – especially in your groin area and hamstrings.
- Wrists.
- Ankles.
- Abdominals.

A combination of Static stretching (pulling a group of muscles and holding them in place) and non-static (such as yoga, or tai chi type work outs) will help start increasing your flexibility. For instance, if you are doing static exercises, you can do a triceps extension stretch, shoulder stretch, chest stretch, core twists, side bends, standing hamstring stretch, butterfly stretch, the splits or a variation of it, ankle rotations, wrist rotations – to name a few (for complete list and detailed descriptions refer to *Martial Arts: Extreme Fitness*). For non-static there are so many asanas or postures to perform, it's best to focus on the ones that will grant you the greatest amount of flexibility. Some of these are cobra/snake, downward dog, the various warrior and crescent poses, half moon, twisting half moon. You must always remember that you are pushing your balance and flexibility with these exercises, keep your head cool, focus on nothing, and just go with the flow.

The most important thing to remember with flexibility exercises is to not over do it. Don't push yourself so hard that you will injure yourself. An hour is perfect. You can do static stretching one day, then non-static the next. Or do only pure static stretching. I gained a great deal of my flexibility by just doing static stretching for an hour, the 4 repetitions for 30 second formula works wonders. Stretching for this period of time is a work out in itself. Stretching is a valuable, very valuable use of time and can save you in a fight or help you win the next tournament.

Strength

The next area to focus on is your strength. There are many things you can do, but at the very least you need to be using resistance for every strike you ever perform. Resistance and Form are the two areas to focus on, get the form down, and then add resistance. The basic technique training involves drilling every single technique you know and focusing on the form, then building up your speed. This can be anywhere from 50 to 200 reps of a certain strike or grapple. After those exercises move on to some heavy bag training or strap on some weights.

Technique training isn't the only thing you can do. Developing your muscles is another critical area for building strength and power. For instance if you can bench press 200 pounds as your toning weight you'll have a killer straight punch or rear cross – greater than if you only toned at 100 pounds. When you go to the gym or work out at home and work every muscle group you'll have a pretty fit body, and be in great fighting shape. These are the critical muscle groups that NEED to be worked out if you ever hope to achieve greater heights.

Chest - Pectoral muscles and Lateral muscles. You will find that the stronger your chest is the more power you'll be able to deliver behind a punch. Bench press, declined bench press, inclined bench press, standing arm raises (in front), standing arm raises to the side, Lateral pull downs (under and over hand), and chest flies.

Arms - Biceps, triceps, wrist/forearm muscles, and shoulders. Your triceps play a major role in the speed and power of your punches; in some punches your biceps are the major group used for power and speed (such as the Backfist). The strength in your wrist determines the effectiveness of your grapples. Most of your defensive moves with your arms use your shoulders, such as parries, or blocks. Exercises like curls, reverse curls, wrist rotations, triceps extension, and the shoulder press are just a few to implement into your training.

Torso - Abdominals, oblique, and lumbar muscles. The torso generates large amounts of power when used right, and when trained right is right out deadly!

EXERCISE

Here's an example, go find a punching bag, or a sparring partner and just hit with your arm. How was it? It probably lacked in power right? Yeah...
Now involve your waist and move your waist as you move your arm. The result, more power! You can put less effort with your arm while using your torso and still have more power. The extra movement produces a far greater amount of power than just your arm.

Sit ups are great, but they will not give you the power you need, and you get that with weight training your core. Weighted side bends, weighted twists, roman chair sit ups, leg lifts, frog kicks and V Sits are really good for building core strength. Just remember, don't work it every day, those muscles need to rest too.

Legs - Quads, Hamstrings, and Calves. Each of these muscle groups play a role in footwork, and of course kicking. Leg press, calf press, leg extensions, hamstring curls are some of the major weight training exercises. Cycling proves to be a great way to build muscle strength in your quads and calves, not to mention the added endurance effect. Of course, my favorite, running, sprinting and jogging when done right can give you tremendous speed on the battlefield. The faster and stronger your legs are the stronger all of your strikes will be.

If we go back to the example of punching in the torso section and add in footwork, the force behind it is staggering. Your arm weighs on average 5% of your total body weight. When you add in your body that's 20 times more mass behind your punch than just your arm, and add in the torque from your waist plus the speed of your footwork, it's incredible! You'll hit someone like a dump truck. This is simply a sound understanding and application of physics! Simple scientific truths when applied yield unbelievable effects on the battlefield.

Endurance

The final area of focus is endurance. We've covered some exercises that can be used for endurance and strength and we'll add to the list. Pushups, cat stretches, pull ups, and other types of non weighted exercises can constitute endurance training. Endurance training is also a philosophy of how you use exercises and how you go about your training routine. For instance if you perform all your weight training back to back with no breaks, that's a form of endurance training. If you do cardio and weight training together, that's a form of endurance training. If you do techniques back to back without breaks, it's a form of endurance training. Anything you do for a long period of time without any breaks can be classified as endurance training. If you can do all your workout routine without any breaks, great! You're just that much better.

Training Program

Now that we've touched on some exercises let's give you a practical routine. Grab something to write with and let's take some notes! I found it most effective to work out in this order. Start with Warm ups, flexibility, core work, endurance, strength training, technique training. You can switch it out, mix it up, do whatever is best for you, but this sequence yields the greatest results the fastest.

A Beginner's Guide - Here we'll look at two workout programs, performed every other day.

Day One

- 2 minutes of warm ups, jumping jacks, running in place, drill through some techniques
- 20 minutes of flexibility, 1 rep of each hold for 30 seconds
- Core work
  - Sit-ups, 2 sets of 30
  - Weighted Side Bends, 2 sets of 30
  - Weighted Twists, 2 sets of 30
  - Frog Kicks, 2 sets of 15
- Cycle for 20 minutes
- Push Ups, 2 sets of 30
- Pull Ups (over hand), 2 sets of 10
- Triceps Dips, 2 sets of 20
- Footwork, running in circles (10' diameter) for 3 minutes

MARTIAL ARTS: Ultimate Warrior   Chapter Three

- Run 2 miles
- Wrist Exercises (weighted, 15 pounds)
    - Reverse Curl, 2 sets of 12
    - Wrist Rotations, 2 sets of 15
    - Wrist curl (over hand), 2 sets of 20
    - Wrist curl (under hand), 2 sets of 20
- Drill Upper Body Techniques for one hour

Day Two

- 2 minute warm ups, jumping jacks, running in place
- 20 minutes of Yoga
- Core Work
    - Leg Lifts, 2 sets of 30
    - Roman Chair Sit ups, 2 sets of 30
    - V sits, 2 sets of 10 seconds
    - Leaning Twist with light bar, 2 sets of 50
    - Good Mornings weighted (15 pounds), 2 sets of 20
- Wall Sits, 1 rep of 5 minutes
- Pull Ups (under hand), 2 sets of 10
- Wide Arm Push Ups, 2 sets of 20
- Footwork, running in a square (10'x10') for 3 minutes
- Weight lifting (Focus on toning)
    - Bench Press, 2 sets of 20
    - Chest Fly, 2 sets of 15
    - Triceps press, 2 sets of 15
    - Biceps Curls, 2 sets of 30
    - Shoulder Press, 2 sets of 15

- o Stationary Rows, 2 sets of 20
- o Weighted Punches, 2 sets of 20
- o Leg Press, 2 sets of 20
- o Calf Press, 2 sets of 20
- o Hamstring Curl, 2 sets of 20
- o Squats, 2 sets of 20
* Run 2 miles
* Drill Lower Body Techniques for one hour

The average time to complete this program is two and a half hours for both days. Which is great! You're getting about an hour and a half of exercise and one hour of actually technique training. This is a great way to begin and then build upon as you're developing strength, flexibility and endurance. You start building a foundation for all the muscle groups that are essential for your journey towards your goal of excellence. For a more detailed program refer to my book *Martial Arts: Extreme Fitness*.

Fuel – The Life Blood of your Training

Now you might be able to follow some of these guidelines in our work out programs but you won't get far without the proper fuel. I've come up with a basic meal guide to help you prepare your body and keep it going once you start your training.

First is a three meal menu, it's pretty basic and you can add things here and there, tuque it to your liking and enjoy.

Breakfast
* Rice based cereal.

- Dried fruit such as bananas, apples, blueberries, strawberries, mangos, blackberries, raisins are additional things to mix in. If you're a nut fan, throw in some almonds.
- Add low fat or soy milk to your cereal.
- On the side have some fresh fruits, such as an apple and a banana.
- Squeeze some fresh juice (pomegranates, oranges and grapefruits make excellent morning beverages), and to add an extra kick to your drink mix in Soy Lecithin Granules (they will help you focus throughout the day).

Lunch
- One Cup of White Rice (unsalted, plain with just water).
- Mixed vegetables stir fried or steamed (green beans, onions, carrots, squash, zucchini, broccoli).
- Lightly seasoned chicken, grilled or baked, or pressure cooked beans (use herbs for flavoring).
- Fruit salad (containing strawberries, kiwi, grapes, melons, berries) of three to five fruits.

Dinner
- One Cup of White or Brown Rice (unsalted, plain).
- Mixed vegetables stir fried (the same or different from lunch).
- Your choice of fish, lean beef (non-processed), or chicken.

- Vegetable salad (dry with no salad dressing) containing spinach, lettuce, olives, cucumbers, carrots, radish, and avocados.
- To mix it up a bit, drink herbals teas every once in awhile.

Here is a six meal program that involves smaller portions. It takes a little more time but it's worth it in results. The advantage to six meals verses three is the fact that your body isn't over burdened by food. Basically you don't have the sleepy feeling after you eat. You will be spreading your meals out every two to two and a half hours. This is great when breaking up your workouts throughout the day.

Breakfast 7:00 AM
- Medium Bowl of Cereal.
- Apple.
- Fresh Juice.

Mid Morning 9:30ish AM
- Small omelet with egg whites (two eggs), with peppers, olives, onions, and meat.
- A piece of fruit.

Lunch 12:00 PM
- One cup of Rice.
- One cup of Beans.
- Stir fried vegetables.
- A piece of fruit.

Afternoon 2:30ish PM
- Protein shakes containing: Soy Milk, 3 kinds of fruits, 3 kinds of vegetables of your choice and protein powder. For starters, pineapple, kiwi, blueberries, spinach, carrots, artichokes.

Dinner 5:00 PM
- Pasta or Rice (one cup).
- Fish, chicken or lean beef.
- Stir fried vegetables (sea weed, asparagus, squash, peppers, beats, green onions).

Evening 7:00ish PM
- Vegetable Salad, or Vegetable Soup (from fresh vegetables).

You may add spices to your meals to change it up so you don't get bored. Paprika is an excellent spice for increasing metabolism. Ginger also helps in losing weight. Soy sauces with low sodium amounts are good for marinating your meats. Sesame seeds are also good for flavoring your meat. Dill is very flavorful and can turn any dish anew. Avoid flavorings that have high sodium levels. Have fun and try out new combinations all the time. The great thing about this program is you don't have to be an expert chef to follow it.

You can mix in and out any of the fruits or vegetables, and the meats; it's really up to you. You can go through a whole week and not eat the same meal twice, just get creative and see what things you want and go for it!

Be sure to drink plenty of water. Anywhere from 90 to 130 oz of water per day is an ideal amount. You'll be sweating like crazy in your workouts so be sure to hydrate yourself. Plan out your water intake every hour, drink anywhere from 8 to 16 oz per time you drink. Drink a glass right before you eat to help fill yourself up.

EXERCISE

Here is an exercise, get out your writing tools. Make a seven day calendar; section out meals either three a day or six a day, or a mix of both throughout the week. Now with the basic guide I gave you, write out your meal plan for the week, try not to make the same meal twice that week, unless you absolutely love it! Then you can have it twice, but only this time! Make it look nice and pretty, and if you have to redo it, type it up, make it colorful whatever, and post it on your fridge. Now for the next seven days follow that menu, stick to it. Eat only at your home; eat only healthy and wholesome foods. If you have to, pre-make a meal and take it to work, or have your spouse or parent or sibling cook it for you and drop it off wherever you are. Trust me when you organize your meals like this you'll soon find out you don't need that much for food, and you might start saving money each month – wouldn't that be nice!

Products

We live in a world where everyone is discovering a special pill, a magical juice, a super formula, you name it it's been capitalized on. Some work, some don't, some are just placebo effects, some are scams, and some legitimate. We're going to talk about the ones that are genuine and that actually have an impact on your health.

Nitric Oxide

> "Nitric Oxide is the molecule of life"
> - Dr Abbas Qutab

Nitric Oxide is a chemical produced in our bodies that helps with every function of the body. Dr Qutab further stated "nitric oxide is a commanding molecule". Without Nitric Oxide the body would cease to function properly. As we get older our bodies start producing less and less nitric oxide. Certain foods we eat produce nitric oxide, blueberries being one of them; however we can't reclaim our once youthful levels of this prized molecule without the aid of a nitric oxide supplement.

Liquid Nitric Oxide is the most potent forms of this molecule, and has many applications, not just for drinking. Liquid nitric oxide can be applied to bruises, wounds, and exterior illnesses. It is the best choice of this supplement because of the ease it has for reaching parts of the body in liquid form.

Picture this. In our bodies we have arteries, blood vessels and other systems to pass along fluids and nutrients. Compare these to the roads or the highways of our bodies. Aging, eating and other bodily functions throw trash onto these high ways. Essentially Nitric Oxide is the "Street Cleaner", and it goes about and opens everything up, allowing nutrients to 'drive freely' on this internal super high way. I don't care if you're putting Italian Race Car caliber nutrients or American Muscle Cars supplements into your body, if the 'road' isn't clear you're not going to have the best results.

When Nitric Oxide is added to your daily regimen of training you'll see a difference in your ability to perform. Your endurance will increase and you will fatigue slower than usual.

Omega 3s and Tocotrinels

Omega 3's are a fatty acid found in fish and some plants. There are also other fatty acids, such as Omega 6's and Omega 12's. Each should be balanced to have a healthy body. Studies have shown that the average American's consumption of Omega 3's is lower than that of Omega 6's. Mainly because of the excess consumption of red meat which is high in Omega 6's. A balance between Omega 3's and Omega 6's needs to occur in order to have a healthy life, and to be able to fully perform at your tip top shape.

Tocotrinels and their benefits have been a topic of recent research. Essentially, a Tocotrinel is a part of the vitamin E family. There are Delta, Gamma, Alpha and Beta types of Tocotrinels. There are also Tocopherols (which have had more common research done), which make up the other half of Vitamin E. Vitamin E is an antioxidant based substance, and is vital to maintaining certain systems in the body. Tocotrinels have a greater antioxidant capacity than Tocopherols mainly because of the slight difference in chemical makeup.

Research in the past few years into the application of Tocotrinels has yielded some interesting results, and the possible treatments could change many people's lives. This is mainly because of the slight difference between the chemical makeup of Tocotrinels and Tocopherols. Tocotrinels have been used in treating various terminal health conditions for treatment and have shown promising results. Tocotrinels are also used to lower cholesterol levels, mainly because of the effect it has on liver (which produces cholesterol in our bodies), suppressing the enzyme that creates it.

There has been research done in the field of combining these two nutrients together, producing a "super" Omega 3 supplement. When used together, the Tocotrinel enhances the Omega 3 fatty acid.

Muscle Repair Formulas

There are a lot of drinks out there that use various substances, such as electrolytes to help restore energy to your body. Over the years I've tried different drinks and found a couple to be pretty reliable. The most effective type of drink is a muscle repair formula, something you can take immediately after your workout to help your muscles recover. I used one brand in particular that worked wonders, and after my long 6 hour workouts I felt like I hadn't done any rigorous training shortly after I used it. It was perfect, it's ideal for anyone who is training right before a competition, or that doesn't want to be burned out after their long and strenuous workout program.

Here are a couple guidelines to picking the right drink. The formula has to focus on carbohydrate based repair, combined with some protein (the ratio must lean more towards carbohydrates, 2:1 minimum ratio). It must also contain essential Vitamins and antioxidants for muscle repair and to prevent soreness from free radical damage.

Daily Inspiration

Now getting yourself into a routine can take some work. You might have to break through some mental barriers, rearrange your schedule, change your life style, you name it. Some might be hard, others not. It takes determination and some will power.

Let me relate a story, and it might resonate with you. When I was younger I was tired of being fat, not just a little over weight I mean obese! I was 80 pounds overweight and I finally decided to do something about it. (Sometimes we have to hit rock bottom before we realize we need to change, it's not good but at least we realize.) It took anger and frustration for me to change. It happened, and it happened fast. I discovered something about myself; anger motivates me to get something done, not malicious anger, but being sick and tired of being sick and tired.

My point is find something that motivates you, recognize that emotion and hold on to it. It will drive you to accomplish the thing you wish to do, and more particularly get into the ideal fighting shape. More often that emotion will be good, however for others it might be anger, frustration, sadness, guilt, shame, or any other negative emotion. If it is negative, turn it around. Focus the energy behind it in a positive way.

- **Never give up!** Always push through, you might think, oh this doesn't work. But let's compare your training to a seed. Does a seed bring forth a plant immediately? No, it takes time, it needs to be nurtured before it starts to take root and grow. And even when the plant sprouts it still needs to be nourished until it's strong. You have to be diligent in your training, set realistic expectations. You don't expect a tomato plant to bear tomatoes the day after you planted the seed do you? Of course not! You set your goals, you know what's best for you, you know your limits, stick to it, and do it! You can do it, I did it, and I bet I was in worse shape than you (I don't say that to brag I say that to empower you. To raise your self esteem and your belief in yourself).

- **Set Realistic Goals.** When you're starting something out, especially anything that has to do with your health, you have to realize where you are, and where you want to go. If your final destination is too much of a leap, break it up into small steps. If you want to do 100 Push Ups in 1 minute, and you can only do 20, set your mini goal for 30. The majority of why people quit is because they do not set reasonable goals, either too easy or too hard. You need to find your perfect stretching point, and as often as possible, measure yourself and ask "can I stretch more?" You're not going to take one leap to the top of Mount Everest; you have to take a bunch of little steps to reach the top. Always remember your training is the exact same way.
- **Belief System.** This goes along with the previous two. In order to succeed you have to get your mind in the right place. More often than not when you start you're not in the right place, but you're heading in the right direction. So you need to do things that will help reinforce your belief in you and your abilities. If you have to start small, but as you begin to learn how to shift your belief system (one thing we'll talk about in detail in Chapter Six) it will get easier and easier to make bigger shifts in your beliefs.

EXERCISE

Let's close this chapter with an exercise. Find a quite spot, relax and get comfortable. Visualize in your mind (if you want you can close your eyes) yourself in the best shape you can. Feel what it's like to have that body, that strength, that speed. Take in every emotion, and write down how you feel, what is it like to have that? You have that now, believe it, and make it a reality. You're at your ideal weight, shape, and size. Embrace it and let it go. Whenever you're down, come back to this exercise and do it again – and don't listen to that negative voice in your head (or the ones around you), just take in what it feels to have your ideal health.

Chapter Four
Power of Thought

"The emanation of thought changes the Universe."

The mind is a powerful tool, for good and for evil. We can see this dynamic throughout history, Einstein and Hitler, Napoleon and George Washington, Robert the Bruce and Edward the Longshanks (i.e. King Edward I of England), Alexander the Great, Vladimir Lenin, Caesar, Genghis Khan. These people demonstrated that the power of the mind can manifest many things. Thoughts are powerful, if we think about something enough it will happen. We'll do something to make it happen or we'll attract it somehow into our lives. Thoughts can have powerful impacts on us.

In the Martial Arts our state of thought is essential, in our training, on the mat, or in real life combat. What we think in a fight determines the outcome. Thoughts of victory produce emotions of joy, satisfaction, happiness, and fulfillment. A thought of loss or of perplexity in a situation causes emotions of fear, hopelessness, anxiety, and paranoia. When we control our thoughts we control our emotions, our actions and over all the result. Understanding this simple formula can shift everything for you! Your life will change not only in your martial arts, but ever other area where you apply this formula.

Throughout this chapter we will discuss the effect of thought on various things, from combat, to self development.

Words and Thoughts

The power of the word is remarkable. Words have the ability to paint pictures in your mind and conjure up new thoughts. Words are the stimuli of thought. Thoughts create words. Thus building an eternal cycle to create new thought or extract old ones, and to spew out thoughts in the form of words.

Thoughts are the projection of our essence. Everything we are emanates at this level. Often our thoughts lead us to action, either to act upon or not act upon the thoughts we are having. Think about the last time you wanted a particular meal to eat. Did you go eat it? Or find a way to have that meal? More often than not you probably got that meal. If not you still probably had a plan to go get it. See, your thoughts lead you to action. Thoughts are influenced by words and vice a versa. Another influence is thought to thought. These thoughts interact with each other to create new ideas, projected actions, words or just more thought. Thoughts can take the form of imagines or sounds within the mind. Sometimes thoughts are produced in words, and to illustrate my point, you're probably hearing these words in your mind as you are reading them, right?

Thoughts have a physiological reaction in our bodies. For instance, if a man is thinking about a beautiful woman he'll become physically aroused. Thoughts produce chemical reactions in our bodies. A thought of fear can produce a physical reaction of shaking. Emotions are determined by thought. The things we think about in any situation result in an emotional response. If you get nervous before a job interview, your will probably have some thoughts of something bad happening or a worst case scenario right before your nervousness. In contrast if you love skiing and are over joyed when you're on the slopes, you will probably have thoughts of an exhilarating time flying down the mountain as you ride the lift to the top. To tame your emotions you must first tame your thoughts.

The Ultimate Warrior uses thoughts and words to their greatest potential. He or she invites the grand governing principles of the universe to govern his or her life, thus shaping their thoughts. This in turn shapes their entire life. They manipulate thought to serve to their advantage on and off the battlefield. To control thought is to control oneself.

Words are the physical manifestation of certain thoughts. We can explain words as the means of delivering our thoughts to others in the physical world. Human beings are not able to use telepathic communication commonly; therefore the human body has a means of moving thought from one mind to another - Words. Once you understand this concept, that words are vehicles of thought, the plane of "thought combat" becomes visible. Certain words paint certain pictures in your opponent's mind. A basic understanding of these words will greatly improve your ability to fight on the battlefield and up your chances of survival or victory.

Certain words have a positive impact on our lives, and on the flipside other words can be devastating. We mentioned earlier the Kotodama and that there is a 'spirit' behind words – for good or for evil. Words in combat paint mental imagines on your opponents mind. Words can be used as weapons in combat. Whereas words exchanged in a loving relationship are often reflections of those tender emotions. Words can swing both ways, and so can Thoughts.

Take a moment and *Imagine* a ravine, and then a road that runs across connecting the two sides by a bridge. One side is your mind; the other is your physical world (the receptacles of Thoughts and Words). The traffic between both sides is the thoughts and words produced by your Mind and your external world – each intermingling with the other side, crossing the bridge to the Town of Physical and the City of Thought. This traffic we will label ideas, concepts, notions, etc. There is an exchange between both the town and the city, the city being more abundant with traffic. However the tiny bridge can only move so much traffic at a time. This analogy paints a picture of what our minds and bodies are like. We all have a means of delivering new thought to our brains, and delivering our thoughts to others. This bridge is the target of psychological warfare in hand to hand combat. Conquering of the bridge means total and complete control of your opponent's City of Thought. You are monopolizing their means of nourishing their Metropolis. Once controlled, the "City" will then produce results of your choosing (such as your victory in combat). This is the basis for In-Combat Brainwashing.

If your opponent's mind can be laid siege to, then would not your mind be at risk also? That is a logical assumption, and a true one at that. Therefore in this part of the current section we will explore the defensive strategies of protecting your 'bridge'.

The taming of thoughts has been mentioned throughout this book. Taming is another way of saying filtering. We *tame* our thoughts by filtering what we allow into our mind. We must control our own bridge between our outside world and our inside world (our Mind – the receptacle of thought). It must be protected at all cost. This vital area of the body is just as important as any other organ that is exposed to physical combat. The *mind* must be defended by its own set of "Blocks", "Parries", "Deflections" and other defensive means. Filtering and determining what we do with 'intruders' (the weapons used on the plane of thought) are these defensive measures.

In order to fully protect ourselves we must understand what is and is not harmful to our minds. The two methods of defending our minds are;

completely avoiding situations that would invoke negative or harmful thoughts, and setting up 'protocols' for unexpected situations that would result in an attack on the mind.

To *avoid situations* one must set up standards or rules for themselves. These guidelines are of things to do and not to do. For instance if you want a certain level of purity in your life you will avoid places and situations that would threaten that purity. If you want to stay sober, stay away from the bar – yes that is a very obvious answer, and so are the rest of the answers for any other example. Avoiding dangerous situations that would plague your mind are obvious. This is the simplest way to protect your mind.

This second method, the setting up of *protocols to dispose* negativity is not as simple as avoiding harm. You must choose to dispose of the negative word or thought that your enemy is using to penetrate your mind. There is a conscious effort at first, and in accordance to the Three Steps to Perfection in Chapter Two, your protocols will become completely automated – the choice being exercised subconsciously.

EXERCISE

So what do you do with the negativity when it hits you? How do you counter? Let's talk about a couple of ways that we can deter and block negative based words and thoughts.

> **Decide How to React** - This step is an underlying principle to protocol. You have must already chosen before hand, how you will react to certain attacks on your mind before any attack ever occurs. Without this foundation you will be reacting haplessly. Go to a place where you can be alone and where you can open up. Close your eyes and with the energy of your soul decide that you

will react in a defensive way against your opponent's attacks on your mind. This is the first step, now let's move on.

Reservoir of Declarations - For those who have trained their mind correctly, in supplying healthy statements for their mind to digest they will find that these statements act as a deterrent to negativity. Throughout this book you will be compiling a list of these statements, or perhaps you already have a bunch written down. These affirmations confirm in your mind and shape it to counter act the negative words thrown at you on the battlefield.

Predetermined Response - Using certain incoming negative words as a trigger for your own In-Combat Brainwashing techniques. This is a type of 'Mental Offensive Defense'. In a training environment you might have the word repeated to you by an audio recording, responding with your own In-Combat Brainwashing technique. Eventually you must be able to cut off the incoming mental attack with your own. These phrases do not have to be the same for each negative word thrown at you. Think of this as physical combat. Are you always going to use a forearm block for every straight punch thrown at you? No!

Earlier in Chapter Two in revealing In-Combat Brainwashing we pointed out that commands have an effect on your opponent's mind. Commands have an inhibiting effect on the human mind. There is a sense of force behind "You better go clean your room or else!" On the contrary, if you were to hear "Let's go clean your room together", there is no force but gentle guidance. The resounding command suppresses and puts pressure on the mind of person on the receiving end.

Purely from a self defense aspect, the use of commands can save one's life. The inhibiting effect of a command when used on an attacker creates a stumbling block in their midst. Commands when used with the correct tone of voice produce the most powerful verbal tool on the battlefield. In our Academy one of the tools we use in self defense is that of commands along with a strike or movement. Every person who studies self defense knows this, that when a command is given the opponent seems to drop to the ground a lot easier than just simply executing the movement.

To go beyond, a negative based command will most surely topple your opponent. Negative based commands can be overwhelming. Emotions such as anger or hate are used to carry the negativity into the mind of the victim. These types of Negative based commands should only be used in dire circumstances. They are part of that Monster you might have to become. In no way should this knowledge be misused. Justifying this type of command can constitute only a few situations – the taking down of a madman, the defending the life of yourself or others. These negative commands are like "fighting fire with fire".

Our actions affect the world around us. If we choose to go to a Movie we in turn stimulate the entertainment industry. One, we support our local movie theater (we pay for a portion of the employees' wages, the manager, the overhead expenses, etc.), we give a profit to the creator of the movie and the actors. By watching the movie we'll create an opinion and most likely share that opinion with others, for good or for ill. All this from the thought "I should go watch…" A very simple thought can change the world.

Words and Thoughts are the two initializing forces that can change your personality, your perspective, your physical and social status, and the people around you. When you control your thoughts and your words you control your world. You control the battlefield. You are its Master, its Lord.
Correct thoughts will lead you to a perfect harmony between your body, mind and spirit. Once harmony is made within your body, then your mind is unlocked, your spirit soars to new heights and you move along the path to ultimate perfection.

Thought Projection

We know how powerful thoughts can be on ourselves, and the world around us, the next step is getting our thoughts out of our head and into the minds of others. I won't go into too much detail, but just scratch the surface of thought projection.

Have you ever felt someone looking at you? Or perhaps when you've been staring at a person from behind them they've turned around quickly to face you? It happens to me all the time when I'm driving in my car. I look at the car next to me and more often than not the person I'm looking at looks back in a quick startled motion. Now it isn't anything malicious, I'm just looking at them and thinking "what are they like?" "Why did they pick that car?" – Thoughts of that nature. Some disagree; some don't believe that a transfer of thought is possible. We're not to the level where we as humans can communicate telepathically, but from time to time certain people can touch the minds of another.

Over the years I've come to understand a little about this subject. From my own personal experience I've seen that simply 'shooting' the thought across to the other person connects the thought to their mind. It takes some mental concentration, but the other person picks up on it. It happens often with my wife, I think something and she says it. On a note more towards the Arts, I've been in situations where a thought I've projected onto my opponent causes them to stop for a second, leaving me an opening. It's not been anything major like a Jedi Mind Trick, but it's had results here and there.

One of the best ways to describe this "shooting" of a thought is that of a projector. Your brain is the source of the thought, and your eyes or even your "third eye" act as the lenses of the projector. Imagine that your thought is being transferred like the light of a projector, instantaneous and precise. You are shouting your thought, within your mind, loud enough so that everyone that makes contact with you hears it. Your eyes are an effective medium for transferring you thoughts, it's often said "the eyes are the window to the soul", and this I've found very true in projecting thought. In a way this helps amplify the thought projection process.

I know some people who don't even belief the notion, and completely shut it out from their minds. Some people just can't understand it, or have no ability to do it. Perhaps it's a talent certain people are given, or an area of the brain that has developed more than others. Whatever the reason why some people can or can't use this ability hasn't been made definite to me, and it's still open to speculation.

The main purpose of thought projection is to build a desired emotion in the other person and manifest it. The words probably will not be heard, but the message gets across. The emotion you desire to instill in your opponent manifests. Thus, accomplishing the result of thought projection. Remember, thoughts cultivate feelings or emotions. Emotions when used correctly act as a weapon against your opponent.

Another variation on thought project is the concept of Remote Viewing. Remote Viewing however has ties back to ancient Japan and China. The process of remote viewing is to simply move one's consciousness to another place. There are various methods of practice and we won't cover all of that in this section, but to point out that remote viewing is a form of thought projection. If one is able to project their consciousness to another place in time and space, then the theory of projecting thought onto another individual ought to apply by the same if not similar rules and laws. For those of you who know how to use remote viewing the theories I've put forth on thought projection can be easily understood and applied.

Mental Penetration

The idea of penetrating someone's mind is a mystic notion that's been around for centuries. From the local psychic hotline, to the gypsies of Eastern Europe, to the ancient oriental spiritualists, the idea is similar. Penetrate the mind and exploit it. During my time in Eastern Europe I encountered some Gypsies on the street. I didn't understand what they were saying and just walked on; my wife was tugging at me and telling me "let's go, now!" I asked my wife what the big rush was, and she explained to me who they were and what they were doing. The gypsies use a similar technique to what I found in certain Asian martial arts. They are able to lure and probe the minds of their victims, thus allowing them to take their money, or belongings without them truly realizing what had happened until after they were long gone. Some might call this a 'waking trance'. From what I understand they use a certain level of tones in their voices, combined with words to open up your mind, and for the individual that is easily persuaded they fall victim to their trap. However this process isn't a fool proof weapon, as you can see from my story I didn't understand a word they said and there was no effect, thus my speculation on the matter is that the human mind can only be dominated by another when it understands and allows the dominator presence in their mind.

A more realistic means would be the use of In-Combat Brainwashing. The whole idea behind it is to penetrate the mind of your opponent and cause them confusion, disbelief, doubt, fear, and all other types of emotions that will result in mental domination. Mental Penetration is not just getting into someone's mind, but to lure them into your trap, make them question, open up and then exploit them. The greatest marketing minds understand these principles, it all stems down to this, grab their attention long enough for them to see, hear, and question.

We'll focus on questioning for the majority of our time here. In the battlefield you have an arsenal of tools; your fists, your legs, the things around you, and then the hidden weapons not visible to the human eye, your thoughts and your words. Often most martial artists or fighters in general, forget this last group of weapons. To them it's all about the kick, the punch, the jab, the knock out. There is a mental battle that is played out here, a battle not looked upon by many, and studied by few.

The battle of the mind starts the moment hostility begins, not when the first punch is thrown, but when feelings are exchanged between participants, when glances are shared, and when a presence is felt. You can prepare for this battle by always being on guard, ready in your mind to strike out not with your fist or foot, but with thought. Your thoughts will lead you through the battle. If you have thoughts of victory intertwined with strong belief in yourself you'll win, and that will be reflected onto your opponent. Now you can always begin the match, or the battle, by throwing thought around, aimed directly at your opponent, penetrating your thoughts deep into their mind, sending messages such as "I am the victor, you are nothing!" "I am unstoppable; you cannot stand up to my speed and strength!" Penetrating phrases like this and others are just a few of the ways to win on this side of the battle. Most likely your opponent will be going over strategy in their mind, thinking of what they can do to stop you since they studied your footage, or saw you in another match, or in another fight on the street – they won't be starting a mental battle, let alone even acknowledge there is one going on. They are helpless victims to your onslaught of thought.

I've used these type of mental penetration techniques frequently in all of my serious bouts, either on the street, or on the mat, and I've always won. Never at any time have I lost when using mental penetration techniques. Let's outline a simple formula for learning how to do and apply this.

Number 1: Develop predetermined phrases of thought. Your first step is to come up with phrases you want to impress upon the minds of your opponents, such as the ones I listed before, or others. Write down 10 phrases, you can include the ones I've shared with your or others that come into your mind.

Number 2: Practice in your drilling of techniques. As you practice use these phrases in your head as you strike, grapple, etc. You do this by visualizing in front of you where you want it to go, into your punching bag, the shield your buddy is holding, whatever it may be, focus first on your thoughts going there, then your hit.

Number 3: Try it out randomly. As you go about your day, and see things or people, test it out, throw your thoughts to them, not to the intent of starting a fight, but to practice real world what it's like beforehand (perhaps you'll deter a fight from happening in the first place).

When you start practicing this, it's going to become second nature. You'll be walking down the street and notice a situation that could be hostile and you'll start projecting these thoughts. As you get better at moving your thoughts to others it will have a penetrating effect on them. They'll look towards you with a startle; raise an eyebrow, the typical "what's that" reaction. In combat your opponents will have a sense of uneasiness that you can play on with your thoughts and physical attacks. This opens up everything for you to play with their mind and mess with their head a little.

Questioning your opponent is another form of Mental Penetration outside that of Thought. When asked a question your mind works to find the answer. The subconscious mind looks for it and brings it up to the forefront of your mind. Certain tone inflictions can cause emotional responses and sometimes a different answer to the same question. A harsh angered tone results in a defensive, perhaps even timid, response.

When in battle, the war of the mind is best fought by questions. Questions lead to search, which can result in doubt, perplexity, and fear. However it can result in reaffirming belief. For the trained mind, questioning by your opponent can be more of a help than a hindrance. In order for this type of penetration to work, the right questions must be asked with the right tone. This varies from person to person, however if one follows the basic steps of In-Combat Brainwashing results can be achieved.

Trancing

The idea of a trance is to put you in a state that's unshakeable. You, in your mind, think that you are unstoppable, invincible, all powerful, and that nothing can deter you. What I call trancing is being able to put your mind in a state that you have one goal, and one goal only, victory! Not a berserker rage, but a calm, cool, tranquil state, ready to take on anything that comes your way. Everything is blocked out; there is nothing that can faze you, and nothing that can distract you from the task at hand. The only thing that exists is the fight or the match.

Trancing is not about malicious rage, it's about being focused. The ability one has to put themselves in a trance determines on the focus level of the individual, their ability to control their emotions, and their amount of practice.

Here are some simple steps to develop your trance.

Number 1: Focus visually in your mind. Here is your first exercise in trancing;

EXERCISE

Sit down in a quite area and focus on a key phrase, "I am unstoppable", repeat it over and over in your head for 10 minutes. The focus of this exercise is to get you to focus on one thing only. As you keep doing this process for these type of phrases they will become set in your mind.

Number 2: Come up with a trigger. In order to use this technique to the fullest, you need to come up with a trigger; it can be a phrase you say to yourself, a snap of your fingers, whatever, something simple and rare. It needs to be something special. Here's an example, you could close your eyes for 5 seconds then open them quickly to a wide-eyed position, not only is this rare, but it gets you into the mood.

Number 3: Use your trance when you're training. The best way to blend this into your style is to practice with it. By doing this you not only ingrain it into your head, but also establish a mental link between martial arts and your trance.

Number 4: Coming out. Just like a trigger, you need a "shut off" switch. It can be anything, such as a simple sigh of relief, or a closing of your eyes. Do whatever is most natural for you in calming yourself down.

Within your trance say things either to yourself or out loud that reaffirm the trance. This coincides with the previous things we've talked about in this chapter. These statements help to anchor in the trance and keep you focused on the battle. When these are repeated over and over you also begin to impress these thoughts upon the minds of the person you're fighting. In a way the trance serves a dual purpose.

Trancing is almost like a split personality, but one that you can control and that is as focused as a laser beam. We'll talk about mental detaching later on in this book and trancing plays a major role in being able to do that. Being able to detach mentally and trancing are two different practices, but can be used together to create a powerful force.

Having this 'dual personality' can be very helpful. Not only does it have the key components for winning a fight, but its less stressful on your over all mental being and health. Think about it, would you want to be in fighting mode all the time? Or would you rather have a switch that you can turn on and off which is just as potent? I'd take the later and it's just as effective, trust me I've tried both and by far this is the best way to go.

Chapter Five
Strategy

"The Strategy of Infinite Flowing Strategy prevails above all."

In combat Strategy is everything. I don't mean rote Katas, I mean solid principles that you can base everything off of. For instance Broken Rhythm (which we covered in Chapter Two) is a strategy, and when applied is one of the most effective ones to boot!

Here is a mind shifting strategy – don't look at fighting as two dimensional, it's not all on one level plane. It's all over, up, down, sideways, diagonal, every direction you can think of, from any position you can think of! (Granted not every position will yield the most power, but you can still beat the crap out of someone if you're launching an assault from the ground.)

Today you will discover useful and effective strategies for the battlefield.

Ground Combat

My whole concept for ground combat came during a training session when I got knocked to the floor during a sparring match. I went on to further develop the concept and came up with this. You can attack with any technique on any plane, on the ground on your back, on your feet, in the air, whichever it may be. It's perfectly fine to throw a straight punch when you're back is flat on the ground, or when you're air borne. To me and my opponents surprise I was able to attack vital areas just as well as on the ground as I would on my feet. In fact the way techniques were thrown completely caught them off guard, yielding another advantage to this strategy.

Here is my observation: People don't expect a punch to come straight up from the ground, or a kick to come up and hit them in the head while you're beneath them. In addition to grappling, punches and kicks can be adapted to hit your opponent while on your back. For instance; when right beneath your opponent you can launch a straight punch to your opponent's groin, or to their inner thigh to knock them off balance. In the same situation you may arc up on your shoulders and perform a hook kick from behind to the back of your opponent's head (if you're right under them they can't see your legs, you'll be in their blind spot).

EXERCISE

Here's an exercise; lay down on the ground on your back. Begin moving side to side, rocking from one side to the other and hold it. Now try throwing a punch or two. Next start to kick, utilize the ground to get momentum on your movements. Shift from one side to the other to start developing your "backwork" (synonymous to footwork). These are simple steps and it gets more complex as you keep developing yourself.

> **Backwork:** The movement of technique delivery when one is lying on their back.

"Backwork" is the main principle for this type of ground combat, and in order for you to maximize your power on the ground you have to master this. Start here with your back and add strikes and grapples as you go.

Transitioning from your back to your feet is essential, if it takes you forever to get back up and your opponent can snap to their feet, ground combat is almost useless. There are various ways of getting back up, rolling up onto your feet, using your hands to push you up, or spinning to gain momentum.

Here's something simple – Ground Combat is like break dancing! Visualize a break dancer. See how they smoothly move on the floor and transition from their back to their hands, or their back and to their feet. They spin with ease. They're fluid, right? Of course, they use momentum to continuously dance.

In my experience I've seen that in the area of real world combat, some if not most martial artists lack in this aspect. Once they hit the ground it's over. So many styles and schools only focus on situations when you're on your feet (if you're studying with a school that does focus on ground combat good!), and there have been a lot of real life situations that turned ugly because someone didn't know how to take the fight to the ground victoriously. So if you want to be a well rounded fighter, not to mention the best in the world, you need to have a solid ground game.

If you don't know any ground game tactics, no sweat! We'll work with you and turn you into a ground combat machine! I've not seen any other school train in ground combat as we do.

EXERCISE

When you're drilling your techniques, once a week you should take it to the floor and drill them on your back and your side, just as you would normally while on your feet.

Study your surroundings

Everywhere you go you need to be aware of what's around. Remember earlier I talked about everything being a weapon in Chapter Two. This and that are two intertwining principles.

EXERCISE

Here's an exercise for you, when you're walking down the street, in the mall or where ever, notice the windows, the beams, railings, pot holes in the road, lamp posts, etc. There's so much to list we could make an entire book out of it! Just do that as an exercise, I'll explain why later.

Just knowing what's where can greatly change the outcome of every battle. Not everyone studies the terrain. In war terrain is a crucial part of planning attacks, fortifying defenses and ultimately victory. In his book *The Art of War*, Sun Tzu gave examples of different terrain, how to exploit it, and what to avoid. (Minford, 2002). This applies not only to military warfare but to hand to hand combat. If you know the lay of the land of everywhere you go, know where objects are that can be used to defend yourself, moveable or immoveable, you will have the greater advantage over any opponent you encounter.

Let's look at a hypothetical example. You don't know the area that well. You don't pay attention to anything around you. You walk into a store and buy your stuff, drop off your mail at the post office in a daze. You're walking around your school campus from class to class, or you're walking around your work place on a break completely unaware. A situation comes up where you have to defend yourself, but you fail to notice the environment around you, you get knocked to the floor and hit your back on part of the curb, damaging one of your vertebrae. Or you're defending yourself and take a couple steps back and trip on a pot hole, lose your balance and whatever you can imagine. It's horrendous!

Now let's look at this situation again, with you knowing what's there. You take your breaks at work, or at school, or walk in a way that you notice and position these obstacles in the way of your potential opponent (now it takes some work, but trust me, when you know and exploit the area around you, a fight on the street won't be so nerve racking for you). With these objects or obstacles in mind you can easily manipulate your opponent into falling into your trap. For instance a simple thrust backward causing them to stumble into a pot hole or off a curb can easily end the fight. You're looking at a twisted ankle, an accidental knock out, or a brief period of time you can use to escape to safety, all without really having to fight.

> "The highest form of warfare is to attack strategy itself"
> - Sun Tzu (Minford, 2002)

In essence you are attacking strategy by exploiting the environment. Their goal is to attack you, mug you, kill you, whatever it may be. They might think they will catch you off guard in an alley or behind a building, but therein lies the attacking of their strategy. You know the area you know how to use it to your advantage, and it topples their overall goal and brings their downfall.

Now whenever you walk into a new place, quickly jot down all the exits and entrances, windows, immoveable objects (such as posts, signs, anchored tables, etc), moveable objects (chairs, plants, tables, books, pens, salt shakers yeah I know it sounds funny but it's useful), anything that can be thrown or used to scare off an attacker, people, animals, etc. With the area sketched out in your head you'll be able to come up with a plan fast. Don't worry your subconscious mind will come up with strategies as you walk around or sit down (If you have programmed it correctly). Just let it do its work.

EXERCISE

Go to a room in your home. Stand or sit whichever you prefer. Focus on one side of the room for thirty seconds to one minute and just stare. Then close your eyes and hold the image in your mind. Close your eyes tight to help retain the image in your mind. Focus your conscious mind on keeping track of what you saw when your eyes were open.

This exercise helps build the 'muscle' in your brain that processes images. The more trained your brain is, the greater the ability to process solutions. Now you don't have to do this everywhere you go. However like all other exercise it is import to do this daily.

Detach, mental bungee jumping

The ancient ninja of Japan used a very sound practice for their warfare. They would mentally detach for specific situations. Now the ninja were masters of disguise, essentially they were actors and actresses, they had to play various roles and hold the composure of that role for long amounts of time.

When studying the ninja and what they were at the core, they weren't blood thirsty assassins. They were a kind, spiritual, and family oriented people. They only took on the guise of assassins when needed, if hired by the feudal lords or the shoguns. They were not a secret society bent on domination and destruction of empires.

In a way most of us, if not all are like the ninja. We're good people at heart. There are a few bad apples in the mix and that's one reason why we practice martial arts. Therefore we do not want to be consumed by our fighting and our matches. We need a tool to use keep ourselves mentally sound, and sane.

One philosophy that I've found to be valuable and that's been time tested is the concept of hanging onto your true self as you dive into combat, or changing a role you must play in order to survive. The best way to describe this is to visualize in your mind you, and attached to you is an unbreakable chain of infinite in length. You jump into a large abyss, as you fall you pass through different roles, an assassin, a host, an entertainer, whatever it is you name it. You stop at various ledges, climb back up to the top, and jump down again and again. But you always return to the top.

The top in this analogy is who you truly are, whatever that may be. For most of us it's a state of a calmness, rest from the cares of the world, peaceful, charitable, showing kindness in our dealings with others, expressing our love to those closest to us. The top is a representation of what we are becoming on our road to total enlightenment, the journey to the mastery of one's self. Sometimes we have to leave our road of enlightenment to deal with current problems in our way, but we always return.

Another way to look at this is a mask. What is the Definition of a Mask?

> **Mask:** An article of clothing used for concealment or protection, also sometimes used in rituals or in entertainment.

Let's break that down, concealment or protection. When we detach we're concealing our true self, thus protecting our true nature. This way we do not taint our true selves in combat. A mask allows us a physical medium to take on various roles, or help get us into the mood of character. A mask is a tool of deception.

Masks can play a role in various principles we've discussed in this book, from In-Combat Brainwashing, Mental Penetration, Various Mindsets for combat (which we will discuss later on) to anything else. The idea of putting on a mask can easily help one transition. It's merely a vehicle to help you detach.

Whether it is a mask or a bungee cord, or another form of detachment, the principle is the same. We do these things to keep our core essence pure. We are not monsters at heart; we only take on the persona of one from time to time, if ever. We are Martial Artists from time to time, but at the very core of things we are after all human beings, progressing and advancing.

Mindset for combat, split personality

Having the right mindset ties directly back to the strategy of detachment, and in a way is an extension of the strategy. It is focused on how we detach for combat.

The goal is to establish a mindset for fighting only, a mask if you will for when you jump into that abyss. We covered some of this in Chapter Four in various sections, but we will focus on specific attributes needed, and how it all works.

Preparation...

Number 1: Recognize when to use it. As you go about your life you will start recognizing what's hostile and what's not. In combination with a trigger to activate a trance or mask or mindset you'll learn when and where to dive into this mental state.

Number 2: Undergo plenty of training. Ideally you will want 1,000+ hours of combat training with the mindset before you even try to use this in a real situation. By doing this you'll have a higher success rate in pulling off the mental dive. Start by putting yourself into that mindset with a trigger.

Number 3: Meditate with this mindset. Find a quite place and meditate with the intent to do battle and come out the victor. In your meditation, visualize actual combat. See yourself in that character for every second. Start out by meditating for five minutes at a time and build it up. Half an hour is a practical amount of time to spend in this type of meditation.
By subjecting yourself to meditation in this state you will be better able to stay in this mindset for longer periods of time, and you will be able to control yourself from going into a rage when you put it to practical application.

Actual Use...

Number 1: Use your trigger right before your fight. Right before a fight breaks out, if you're exchanging words, "jump off the edge". In real combat you don't want to wait until after the first punch is thrown. It's too risky and there is a possibility emotions will get in the way.

Number 2: If using in sport... Depending on what type of competition you're in you might want to shield your true potential until you absolutely need it. Play it as your trump card. I've done this a lot in sparring matches and tournaments where I needed something to pull me out of a tight spot.

We established in the previous chapter the theory of trancing. This current topic is a more focused tactic of having a specific trance. You can have one for pure self defense, you can have one for street fighting, and one for competitions. One way to distinguish between various trances or mindsets is to use "keywords" to activate each trance – a Kotodama.

Essentially you set up a "persona" for whichever you desire. It's really up to you. Pick the attributes you want and build that personality. For any of you actors or actresses out there, you're building a character, and you're getting "into character".

My street combat persona has attributes such as a deeper voice, using in-combat brainwashing to instill fear into my opponent's mind, looks that cause someone to tremble, an "evil grin" to help instill that fear. For me, that persona is about fear, inflicting fear into my enemy and proving in words, actions and thought that I am the superior one in the battle and they will lose and suffer.

My Competition persona is one of quite determination, a look in my eyes that cuts to the soul. I am an unquenchable fire encased in a small furnace, and when opened unleashes an inferno. I don't say much in my "competition mask", if any words are exchanged it's more or less "I'm ending this now" type of attitude. I have complete and total faith in myself that I will win. I am a little arrogant in this persona.

My Self Defense persona can be pretty loud at times. In a basic self defense situation noise is the key to scaring off any attacker. I use many commands with my movements, and it's all about protecting not just me but my opponent. The core principle behind this is to stop them in a way that I don't get hurt and neither do they. In this persona I have quite a bit more charity than my street fighting persona.

There are many other personas one can build besides these, and these are only for martial arts. I have other mindsets that I dive into, the Marketer, the Trainer, and other various roles I have to fill – Excluding being a friend, a husband, and a father. Those are things that stay on the top, and where your true self should come out and shine the most.

To sum up this strategy, we can compare it to armor. Imagine every time you leave your comfort zone, your home, your loved ones, you put on your armor, "you jump off that cliff". You might need a sword and shield for one situation, a bow and arrow for another or two swords. There might be places where chainmail might do better or a full plate mail. Every situation is different, and not one mindset will work for every situation. Adaptability and Flexibility are two important attributes you must have when applying this strategy to real life. You must be able to adapt, move in and out of various personas or masks at a moment's notice. Life comes at you fast, even faster when you're a martial artist.

Attack the weapons

I was in a sparring match in 2001 and made a wonderful discovery. I came in with a low punch to my opponent's stomach when he blocked with his knee, I hit him in a spot that caused him to tumble to the ground (on his shin mind you). It caused a lot of pain. I was sure I hit a pressure point. After that experience I began toying with the idea of striking one's arms and legs. To my surprise it was an excellent strategy.

The typical martial artist expects to get hit in the chest, the stomach, the head and maybe the upper thighs. They don't however expect to get hit in the arm as their punching, or the legs as they kick. Perhaps this is a mental 'glitch', if you will, that since certain people don't expect a strike to their weapons their mind isn't prepared to handle the pain – thus the appearance of more pain. However certain points in the body do feel more pain than others (such as pressure points, nerve endings, etc). Areas with less fat and muscle tend to hurt more when struck than areas protected with those tissues.

Attacking your opponent's weapons can prove quite potent. In later cases I noticed that attacking my opponent's arms often created huge gaps in their stance. And with an unguarded center line it was a lot easier to overpower them. It has a great tactical advantage.

Some styles of self defense focus on striking or grappling a person's wrists who wield a knife or pistol – the whole point of that idea is to disable the weapon and take it out. And when someone doesn't have an external weapon, the next thing would be to take their arm out of commission or their leg. It's not a wise choice, but in some situations it might be needed, the disabling of your opponent's arm or leg could result in some major damage, most likely permanent, and probably a lawsuit on your end.

The main purpose for this strategy is to either;
- Create an opening for you to launch an assault, or
- Cause enough damage to get them to give up or run away without causing any serious harm that would result in legal action against you.

There are various ways to utilize this tactic. Imagine your fist or foot springing into action to impact their punch or kick. Or grappling their weapon of choice and striking with your free legs or arm. And lastly to use what we call at the Academy "Deflections". These are all great ways to apply this strategy, but the best is to have a mixture of all three. The reasons I suggest this are; you keep your opponent unaware of what's happening next, you can use the different ways to attack both their weapons and their core without them knowing which is which (using feigns to confuse them), and they won't be able to effectively counter you moves.

Joint locks, breaks, and dislocations

The use of joint locks, breaks and dislocating joints is a practice over looked in some styles. Various styles of martial arts focus on just strikes. However that leaves a very limited arsenal of techniques. Combat is not about limitations, but ever expanding possibilities. When you add grapples and joint locks, along with certain breaks, you completely change the battlefield.

There are techniques that invert your opponent's limbs. Now it's not recommended to use these, only in dire situations, but if it's your only option and you need to survive then you have to do it! There are quite a few different joint locks and dislocations in many Chinese martial arts, Shaolin being one of them. Joints such as the elbow and the knee are the more common areas to use such dislocations or inverting. However the shoulder joint is another target area. These areas can be used as a sort of submission when used with a dislocating technique – so that if they do retaliate you will invert their joint.

Jujutsu is an excellent style to study to increase your knowledge of joint locks, and grappling technique. In fact I recommend every martial artist needs to have a knowledge not just in strikes, deflective defense (like blocks and parries), but in grappling as well. You're not complete without it. Statistically most street fights go to the ground as a result of using grapples and submissions. If you don't have a grappling arsenal, you're no better off than the bum you're fighting on the street. To expand on that point, you must know how to defend against and manipulate such assaults. Only then will you be fit for survival.

Multiple Attackers

One might think the appearance of two opponents at once is a bit staggering, and the more and more that show up on the battlefield causes greater emotions of fear and doubt. I want to put forth a counter to that argument, and prove to you that when there are two or more people attacking you, you have the upper hand.

The Psychological approach to this situation is that, the person that is ganged up on is in fear, doubt, worry, and in a bunch of stress because of the appearance of two predatorily attackers. The two assailants come on the scene with the impression that because there are two of them the outcome is obviously in their favor. This can only hold true in a normal situation with non trained individuals… sometimes

A factor that isn't taken into consideration here is the 'victim' (so shall we call the attacked) will have a sudden burst of adrenaline due to the increased stress. This could possibly turn the tide of the battle if ended quickly.

But we won't focus on any physical difference in this section. Rather I would like to turn your attention to a mental side. Yes it's all about what's in your head, yet again!

We mentioned before that the two attackers most likely would have the impression that they will win. A result from the notion, 'arrogance in numbers'. This is a flaw that can easily be capitalized on and exploited. The other problems they have all result from this;
- One, they look at you as easy prey,
- Two, they won't use their skills to the best of their abilities, and
- Three, they don't take into account that you've had some training in defending against multiple attackers.

Let me relate a story, and I don't do it to boast, but to illustrate this point of arrogance. Years ago during the time while I was training hard in Jeet Kune Do I suffered some muscle injury due to over doing my work outs. I had strained most of the muscle in my upper back. Some so severely that I couldn't move my right arm for almost a month, and I couldn't lift anything after that for another two months. At a similar time I had attracted some anger in some people and ended up in a scuffle with eight other guys. Now they knew my weakness at the time and decided to take advantage of it. However they didn't take into account that I could do anything with my legs. So I'm in a situation where I can't use my arms, I'm surrounded and I have eight hostile adolescents around me ready to make their move. Lucky for me they had that same kind of arrogance I mentioned earlier. Needless to say the encounter ended briefly and I was able to make my escape without too much damage. I did suffer a few blows to my back which slowed my recovery, but I was the one walking and they were on the ground.

So what happened here that I, an injured guy who couldn't make any use of his arms, walk out almost unharmed and eight hostile muscular dudes are in shambles? Well I understood that when people are in groups, especially in a fight, think they have it made. I exploited their weakness against them, destroyed their strategy. I had full confidence in my abilities. In fact I even look at multiple attackers different than one on one; I think one on one is more difficult. Let me explain why.

When you're in a one-on-one situation you got to deal with eight plus weapons coming at you, and as many as four at a time. When you're dealing with a group of eight people you got sixty four weapons potentially, but very often when people gang up on you only one or two will go at you at a time, and rarely will they try to throw two punches, or a punch and a kick at the same time. So what are you dealing with? Eight weapons still and only one or two at a time. One of the advantages about being in a situation like this is that you can attack from both sides at once. Your arms can be flailing around, and your legs can be snapping into action all over the place! It can be pretty scary dealing with a martial artist trained in defeating group encounters. One, they have the physical skill needed to take the group down; and two; they have the mental skill in manipulating the group. The moment you take out two or three guys at once you turn the emotions around, and instead of being the fearless they become the fearful.

How are we going to get this right in your head? Not sure? Here are some things to think about and mull over in your mind. You might just have a perspective shift on how group encounters actually work.

- **First.** You need to recognize the way people are thinking, refer back to the previous equation. It's still the same amount of weapons coming at you right? Ok maybe it can double but it won't. Your opponents will most likely throw individual punches or kicks one or two at a time. They might attack one after the other, but since you're fast enough it doesn't matter. The strikes might be split seconds apart, but you *can* do a lot in a split second.
- **Second.** You have to look at everything in a minimized time frame. One way to do this is see how many punches you can do on average per second. You do this by drilling a set amount of punches with a timer and dividing the total amount of punches by the time it took to drill all of them. Once you get everything proofed and you see how fast the average opponent can punch you'll be surprised at the numbers. It's simple math! You'll win just by this equation.
- **Third.** You have to realize they're not using their potential and you are. Most of the time people who gang up on an individual lower their use of potential by the amount of people with them. If

there are two they'll probably use 50% each. If there are ten, 10% each. When you truly sit down and do the math it matches up to one person at 100%. And what are you, one person at 100%! What's the difference here? Nothing! You're equal, that's why the more people the easier it gets. When you utilize tactics to get them one on one it's ridiculously easy. Think about it, would you rather fight one person at 100% or ten people at 10%? The 10%!

In *defeating* a group like this you need to be like a whirlwind. You have to be able to use multiple spinning combinations in various orders, know how to shift people's body weight so you can play bowling with them and knock their buddies down, and you need to have the attitude of a ferocious lion. You can even set up a persona or mask for this, heck I did and it works amazingly well. Like I said, *group* encounters tend to be *easier*, at least when you're dealing with a bunch of amateurs.

When you're dealing with a seasoned group of fighters it is a whole new story. How do you know that any of those attackers are no virgin to combat? There are many factors, but some of the basic include; any knowledge about each individual's background, body language they are giving off, feeling out their intentions, their footwork, the way they coordinate themselves as a group, how they strike, their eyes (or the emotion behind them). There is no one tactic in dealing with these types of individuals, each of them will be unique. If some are Martial Artists you will need to know and understand the weaknesses of their style and then manipulate those weaknesses quickly. Careful study of your opponents and the situation before any blows are exchanged is crucial to your survival. Those observations can help you make it out alive and if neglected you will most likely end up dead.

You also need to be on the lookout for hidden weapons. People in groups like to carry knives and guns with them, so be prepared for any surprises by noticing any bulges before hand during your negotiations, and go for those guys first. Taking the armed opponents out at the beginning will surely make things a lot safer.

Disarming

We will not go into too much detail about disarming, but when possible you should use their weapons against them. It's better to use their weapons against themselves than to ever have to pull out your concealed weapon, or throw a punch. The trick is if you're in a position to utilize one of their resources, then utilize it! If you know there is a guy with a gun, disarm them as fast as possible and hold the rest of them at gun point, then call the police station.

Switching Styles

During my early days of studying Wing Chun, in sparring matches I would often throw some techniques of karate into the mix. It would constantly throw off my opponent. I would be all soft one moment, then hard and rigid the next. I was starting to understand key principles that are essential to truly succeed in the Martial Arts. After studying Jeet Kune Do I took it a step further. I purposely designed this strategy to mix in and out of various styles and techniques I had learned. *Weaving* and *blending* everything I know into one all encompassing style, a style of my own. As I kept using this strategy I gained the nickname "Mr. Unpredictable", one sparring partner of mine said "you're too damn unpredictable I hate sparring with you!" He was used to compliance and the uniform system, and to top it off he was a fourth degree black belt in Tae Kwan Do. That goes to show that even black belts don't know everything, it's just something that holds up your pants anyway.

I started analyzing how the different styles can mesh and flow together. In fact I would spend hours in my private dojo practicing shifting from one style to another. It took years to get it down to an effective science. The most important thing in applying this strategy is to not get stuck within style rules and regulations. "Oh, wait I can't kick above the waist", or "That block is too hard". Whatever they are just throw them out for that practice session and hold on to them for later. Those rules are important for other things, so don't kick them out completely; you might need them in a competition one day.

I keep adding to this system today; every time I *learn* something new I jot it down and *record* it for further *study* later. I drill it and compare and contrast it with what I know and have mastered in the past. Each time I go into a sparring match or some unlucky fellow tries to pick a fight on the street I unleash this broken style. It's completely non-predictable, there is no pattern, and it is never the same. This is an ever growing principle, the sky is the limit!

Be relentless

Martial Art is about *combat*, *battle*, and *victory*. You can't hesitate in a fight, or a match or else the other guy will take advantage of it. In other words when someone is hesitating in a fight *you* take advantage of it.

Having charity and kindness are great attributes, but they can prove fatal in a life threatening fight. Speaking more particularly about

street fighting, but it can be applied to the sport side of Martial Arts. Having compassion on your opponent can really devastate you;
- First off, it's a life and death situation, not a game.
- Second, your opponent won't show that same compassion to you; after all they did start the fight in the first place.
- Third, kindness in a fight is a weakness they play on to lure you into a trap

You have to have the fury to take them down and out fast, and leave! Now you don't want a raging volcano of emotion. You want it *focused* enough to get the point across but not kill them or cause serious life changing injury. Being *relentless* isn't about losing *control*, in contrast it's the pinnacle of control. This is one of the greatest forms of control a martial artist can exercise. When you get to this point you start walking a razor thin line in combat. You can't sway either way, the result would be too soft or too out of control.

This strategy is one of the hardest to implement, and takes a great deal of training and preparation mentally and physically. You have to control your mental state to point just before your adrenaline kicks in and hold back your physiological state just before the threshold of a sheer berserker's rage. You won't be able to fully put this to the test at first, but as you work on controlling your emotions through various training exercises (which we will cover in Chapter Eight) you'll start to learn how to control your body and your mind in harmony.

Multiple Strikes, Double, Triple and Quadruple

Not many styles of Martial Arts put forth the strategy of using multiple limbs as weapons at once. Some Katas give certain movements that coincide together, but the idea of free flowing multiple strikes is foreign to most Martial Artists.

Let me ask you a question, is it easy to block or dodge one strike? I'd hope the answer is yes. Here's another. How easy is it to defend against four attacks at once? Whatever the answer may be, the principle of multiple strikes is essential to a "killer" offensive assault.

Double Strike
Now let's discuss the Double Strike. Essentially you're launching two weapons at once. It can either be two punches, a punch and elbow strike, a punch and a kick, a punch and a grapple, etc. You get the point. The purpose of the Double Strike is to confuse your opponent with which strike is the main strike or grapple. In fact you can use the Double Strike strategy as a feign. They both can be feigns for the actual strike you're planning to launch. One of the two might be a decoy. For instance the front and foremost strike being a soft blow and the later being a hard blow. This can cause a psychological blip with your opponent, almost instantly they'll think the other blow is soft and they'll be caught off guard. Not many people use double attacks, some think it's a waste of energy, but I put forth the point that in the long run you save energy because of the energy you put forth up front to end the match.

Triple Strike
The Triple Strike can cause quite a bit of confusion. When you throw two upper body strikes and a lower body strike into the mix you're opponent will not know where to block. Especially when the Lower body strike is low. It's a great tool for distraction. I've never seen a successfully executed triple strike countered. You're bound to get a hit in. They might defend against one or two of the strikes but the third always makes contact. Now a Triple Strike almost always involves one leg and both arms or one arm and the head. Like I mentioned earlier, a Triple Strike, much like a Double Strike is great for distraction, mostly distracting with your upper body to keep your kicks out of sight from your opponent.

Quadruple Strike
The Quadruple Strike is the pinnacle of multiple strikes. There are various combinations but the main addition to this is using your head, literally. This group of strikes works well in a close range situation with multiple people. There is however a principle that alters this, and that's the idea that any strike can be performed on any plane. The one area I'm going to give you (and there are others) is an airborne situation. For instance, let's say that you're surrounded by four or more people. Given there is the correct distance and with the correct speed you can hit your opponents with two punches and two kicks. It takes an incredible amount of effort and ability to perform a strike such as this, but with enough practice and experience it can become a powerful tool. You're probably thinking "How the *$)# do I do that?" "Is that even possible?" I'll tell you what, once you get it down in your head

and study it out, you'll be able to do it in real life. This sets us up for a point we'll discuss later in Chapter Eight, so just hang on to that.

I'll give you a hint; you'll need fluidity in your movements. Everything will come from the core. The easiest way to perform this is to use a type of Straight Punch and Side Kick (or Heel kicks, if you have the flexibility in your legs) combination. You're probably getting the picture right? Yes… The key to this is to do it all while you're in mid air. You might fall to the ground but that's ok. You've just taken the battle to their feet. Go back to a point I made earlier, about break dancing, are you seeing it now? It's a perfect set up to a group encounter.

We mentioned earlier about arms and legs flailing all over the place in the multiple attacker section of this chapter, and I will clarify and expound upon that. In a way that's a form of using multiple strikes; a double, triple or quad assault can go in multiple directions. When that happens you're an explosion of energy and power. Your arms and legs fly around with precision and exactness. It's an ideal way of putting distance between you and your opponents. In fact this is one way to deal with multiple attackers who are surrounding you, even if there are eight guys and four of them throw a punch or a kick at once. You simply react with multiple strikes and grapples.

Multiple Strikes are meant to be unpredictable; there is nothing static about it. It brings in freshness to your style of fighting. It's such a unique way of doing combat that it will definitely catch your opponents off guard. The possibilities with this strategy are incredible! I can't believe all the avenues one can explore with this. You could study and *expand* this for *years* and still have more room to grow – it really is mind blowing!

Chapter Six
Mindset

"The mind is the most powerful tool on the battlefield."

Earlier in this book I gave an example of a boxing match. Which illustrated the point that mindset, or intention is a determining factor in a fight. Throughout the book we've mentioned mindset in different areas, and in this chapter we will be focusing on the correct mindset to have in a battle and how to obtain it. Near the beginning of this book I had you write down something that you thought was powerful (refer to *Power* in Chapter One), so grab those notes because we're going to use them here.

Take out your list and read it out loud. Those are principles or attributes you associate with power. Go ahead and write down everything that comes to your mind right now of what you believe are principles, beliefs, and attributes that make one powerful – or in other words *The Ultimate Warrior*. Just write as your mind pours it out. This is a crucial step; just let it flow without interruption. This list is going to be a part of your foundation for building the correct mind set. *Treasure* this as though it is a *priceless* artifact. Throughout this chapter we will help you apply this list so that all these things become a part of you.

The Mantra

"I am the ultimate warrior. I can never be defeated, all my opponent's fall before me. I triumph in victory. My body is in perfect fighting shape. My speed is unmatched, my strength is limitless, and my techniques are executed with flawless precision. I topple anyone who dares to challenge me. I am relentless in any battle, I do not hold back for anyone. I always win, no matter the situation. I calculate strategies to victory and execute them swiftly as if I always knew them. I adapt to any situation, use any tool, there are no rules. I am fearless. I delight not in war but in victory in war. Numbers are no challenge, wither it be many or few enemies they will fall to my skill and power. I am unmatched in strategy; I see endless strategies on which to exploit my enemies' weaknesses. My defense is impenetrable, yet I penetrate the defenses of others. My reflexes are faster than light. Nothing can stop me! I NEVER Give up! I see the outcome of every battle, every step flows through my mind. I control the battlefield; I am its master, its Lord. The battlefield obeys and I prevail. I am the God of Victory. This is the way of Ultimate Excellence."

This mantra has been one of the core structures of my beliefs in combat. It's been added upon and improved over the years, and is ever growing. The attributes described within it are reflections of what one must become to achieve their perception of the Ultimate Warrior. There is no medal, no physical title, and no rank that displays what the Ultimate Warrior is.

The Ultimate warrior is different for everyone; it's only what you perceive in your mind. However the principles and practices outlined in this book have lead to my ever growing development into what I call the "Ultimate Warrior", and they will surely jump start or enhance what you're doing now. And if we have the same or similar views on what we call the Ultimate Warrior then what you find in this book will be more valuable than almost anything else on this planet.

The Effect of Music

In developing your mindset one of the best ways to do so is to listen to music that has lyrics of what you want to become. Music is extremely influential in building the correct mindset. Now I'm not saying don't listen to any music that doesn't have fighting principles in it. I am saying you need to listen to positive uplifting lyrics (I prefer musical scores without lyrics, but there are some exceptions).

One of my favorite songs is *The Touch*, by Stan Bush. The lyrics of that song are powerful and moving. I always am motivated when I hear it, and the phrases in it have become a part of me. In a way that song is a type of brainwashing, and for me it's healthy to listen to! Those lyrics hold core characteristics of what I associate with the Ultimate Warrior. I took this song further and adapted the lyrics to say "I" instead of "You". I repeat this adaptation when I listen to the song. There is a powerful effect when you have "Double Positive Reinforcement". A deliberate change in wording causes a very interesting psychological effect. You receive positive reinforcement from both inside and outside, thus you start to believe these things faster than the "either or".

In addition to Lyrics, musical composition (notes, cords, "licks", and other components that make music) should also be considered. Music, not lyrics, has a powerful impact on your body and your mind. When choosing music to assist you in your training you must consider both the lyrics and the musical composition. If you don't, it will be like eating a leafy salad, but pilling pounds of pure fat on it before you begin you consume it.

EXERCISE

Pick three of your favorite songs. Analyze the music and the lyrics. Are they uplifting? Do they imbed your mind with powerful images? Does the music build you up?

Music is powerful; rather I should say *Correct* Music is powerful. When applied at the beginning of your training it helps shape your mindset and fosters it in a way that you will succeed and become what you set out to become.

Every time you strike you strike with a declaration

The mantra earlier in the chapter gave various statements outlining what one must become. I found it effective that whenever I'm practicing my techniques I recite this over and over in my head. Repetition with these statements over a long period of time ingrains them deep into your subconscious mind, thus causing you to react with these beliefs. This is one of the best ways to root aspects you want to develop into your mind and your over all being.

Visualize yourself as the winner every time

Whenever you are starting a match or a shadow sparring match, visualize yourself being the winner. Close your eyes and see yourself unleashing the fury of your arsenal against your opponent. Take in what it feels like as you triumph in your mind. Breathe it in and let it all out.

Another way to do visualization is from time to time, close your eyes and see yourself as the winner, or toppling some great obstacle. In our training programs we use the latest technologies in helping our students visualize themselves performing super human feats, defeating opponents and accomplishing any other task that will improve themselves.

Self visualization is a powerful tool to use in growing your belief in your abilities, and making attributes your own.

When you're tired, be your own Personal Drill Sergeant.

One approach I've use in my personal training is to set your mind to a goal or objective and do everything in your power to accomplish that. Wither it be running a mile in under five minutes, doing a thousand pushups, or drilling tens of thousands of strikes. I had my own personal drill sergeant in my mind, coaching me, pushing me to my limits.

When I first started my Jeet Kune Do Training program it almost killed me! The way I was working out and how I compressed it so I could actually fit it into one day was incredible. I don't know why I pushed myself so hard and so fast. Perhaps it was ambition, personal aspirations, a form of pride. However the huge jump in my training paid off. Not only did I have great physical results, but I was able to create a totally new work ethic for myself. All the while I had my personal drill sergeant pushing me.

What is it going to take for you? Well you have to figure out a goal you want to achieve. It can be whatever you desire, just keep that goal in front of you at all times in your mind. If it's in a workout, then start your workout by telling yourself what your goal is, but you have to do it with the right emotions behind it. If it feels like a drudge, start over. Clear your mind, think about your result and then state your goal and get to work.

Sometimes you're going to have to get really angry and just push yourself to the max. If you're body is failing, just tell yourself "No! You're going to do the rest of those sit ups", or "You're going to keep running".

Remember it's all in your head whether you can finish it or not. Yeah your body is tired, but you're just finding the limits of your body. Your body doesn't determine if you can reach your goals or not, your mind does. Just push it! Now there are extremes, and I've learned the hard way, that you can over do it. You need to have a balance between determination and heeding your body's limits.

EXERCISE

It's time for an exercise. Write down the phrase 'I push myself to my limits'. Now instead of using less dominate exercises we're going to do something called VAKS (which means Visual, Auditory, Kinetic, and Spirit). There are four phases to this exercise, and all involve you saying the phrase out loud.

> **Visual** - Bring your arms out in front of you – straight out from your eyes, clasp your hands together and stick both thumbs up. Now make a sideways figure eight with your hands, coming up in the middle of the figure eight. Now without moving your head follow with your eyes your thumb as they makes a sideways figure eight. Repeat the phrase out loud. Repeat the phrase three to ten times.
>
> **Auditory** - Close your eyes and grab both of your ears with corresponding hands, placing the thumbs and forefingers on your ear lobes. Massage the pressure points in your ears up and down as you repeat once. Repeat the phrase three to ten times, stay consistence with the number of times you repeat the phrase for each segment of the exercise.
>
> **Kinetic** - This takes some practice, but you'll get used to it, bend your arms at the elbows and stick your elbows out and up, making your arms perpendicular to the floor and level with your shoulders, keep the palms flat. You perform a corresponding movement

between your torso twisting and raising your legs to meet your palms as you twist from side to side (DO NOT LOWER YOUR ARMS), i.e. your right knee touches your left hand and your left knee touches your right hand. As you move repeat the phrase three to ten times.

Spirit - Close your eyes, and place your hands on your heart, you might start to rock back and forth, that's ok. This segment is meant to help you feel with your heart or your emotions the phrase you are declaring. Repeat the phrase three to ten times, gradually increasing in volume each time. Don't yell, but have a full, firm voice.

I don't care what it is, this works for anything! When you apply this practice to any type of belief you want to build it will work. There is the chance you could have a conflicting belief, which would be like putting both feet on the gas pedal and the break in your car – you won't go anywhere but at least you're not going backwards. It can take time, but as you continue to utilize the practice of VAKS you'll erase those counter beliefs. Then the 'new' principles or beliefs will become core characteristics that govern you life.

Have an "I can do it!" attitude

This goes a long with the previous section. The secret to this is to have a positive outlook on the situations you're in. Don't fall to negative emotions. In fact by changing the way you look at situations with this kind of attitude you'll start to see those emotions shrinking in their appearance.

One way of dealing with situations in a positive way is to have a healthy mindset, and confidence in yourself that you can make it through anything. Remember, "Nothing can stop [you]!" You look at situations with a "How can I fix this…" NOT "Why…"

As you go about your days every now and then tell yourself in your mind positive reinforcing facts about your warrior mind set. Simple reinforcement at anytime is so powerful, and it can drastically change who you are in a matter of weeks or months.

A Warrior's Spirit, Ken-Ki

Ken-Ki is a set of words of Japanese origin to describe a warrior's fighting spirit. It's not enough to have the mind right. You have to have that *spirit* about you. One doesn't wake up and happen to have a fighting spirit about them; it has to come through time, experience and choice. Even after years of experience some people just don't have that spirit about them. I've seen various black belts, professional martial artists, and so forth that don't exude this spirit. They might have some inner game strategies right with them and have great techniques, but they lack the emotional content behind their actions and their words.

Martial Arts is about aligning body, mind and spirit into one, and when that occurs you can do remarkable things on and off the mat. You might have your mind and your body in the right shape, but take out your spirit and you're done for. It's not about practicing martial arts; it's being a martial artist. Going to classes, and learning new things is great, but in order to achieve new heights not discovered you have to put all the energy of your soul into it.

So how do you get this fighting spirit? Well there isn't a "one, two formula" to do the trick. In fact it all deals with you. There's no time table that says, if you do X for Y amount of days you'll end up with a fighting spirit. It varies from person to person. You have to chose, I don't mean say to yourself "I want a fighting spirit"; you have to choose from deep within yourself. Once your subconscious mind and your conscious mind allow you, then that's when the fire begins burns within you. Obtaining your Ken-Ki is a rebirth; you rise like a phoenix from the ashes, never to be the same again. The only way to tell for sure is when you're in your next sparring match, your next street fight, and there is an absolute change about you. It will burn from every fiber of your being, you will feel it consume you, and you will fight like you have never fought before.

Thus when mind, body and spirit are aligned you are an unstoppable force to be reckoned with!

Chapter Seven
Mental Exercises

"The mind is the most important muscle man must train."

We've discussed various exercises you can do, in your mind as well as with your body. However we haven't covered everything yet, and in this chapter we'll go over some training exercises for you to do to further develop your mind as a tool for combat.

Meditation

What is meditation? There are a lot of different definitions out there, some say it's relaxing, calming your mind, tapping into the universe, looking inward at ourselves and evaluating our thoughts, beliefs and actions, shutting everything out and focusing on yourself, or simply pondering life or a particular subject. All these things can be classified as meditation, but we will focus on a specific type of meditation exercise to help you better yourself, and this is what I'll refer to as "meditation".

We'll refer to meditation as a period of time when you put yourself in a relaxed state, allowing certain parts of your subconscious mind to appear and interact directly with your conscious mind. This is a 'base' that we will build on, expanding into other variations or versions of 'meditation'.

Let's outline some effective ways to put yourself in a meditative state, different things work for different people, so try everything out and decide what's best for you;

- Find a quite room that you feel the most comfortable in.
- Turn the lights off.
- Sit down either on something soft or on the floor. If you're sitting cross your legs. You might prefer put your back against something solid to help prop you up.
- You can also lay flat on your back.

- Start to breath in deeply (but not too much), and out.
- Focus on your breath, it helps quite your mind, and that's the goal here. Keep breathing and once you feel you have cleared your mind of every other distraction you're there. It helps to close your eyes as to not focus on anything in particular.
- To bring yourself out, bring your breathing back to normal, open your eyes and look around.
- Do something to bring you back to the room and the present time, but do it gradually.
- Don't jolt yourself out of your meditative state.

Some of the benefits of meditation include; a calmer perspective on the world around you, your mind gets to "dump" all the garbage from the day – it's like hitting the reset button on your mind. You will be more focused on whatever you do after (therefore it's good to meditate before a tournament, a test, or even a regular training exercise), it prevents nervousness before those "big events", and you feel a lot better!

Additional Meditation Exercises

Self Visualization - We've talked about self visualization earlier in this book, and it's a powerful tool, but even more powerful during a meditative state. Imagine the power of visualizing yourself in a pure, calm and collective state of mind. Just think of the improvement you will make, how rapid your progress will increase. Isn't it satisfying? Yes!

Drilling Technique - While meditating; once you've cleared your mind begin to practice all of your techniques, drilling them over in your head. Visualize yourself doing it from a distance, checking the form. Then move to a first person view and feel every movement, feel your muscles moving as you strike or grapple.

Sparring - You can take this exercise a bit further and perform a sparring match, which we'll explain more in detail in this next section.

Goals - One of the greatest things to do when setting goals is to visualize yourself there. Doing this in a meditative state cements this in your mind and gives you a sure direction to follow. Your mind knows exactly what it needs to achieve, what it needs to look like, and will help you create and follow plans to get to that point.

Auditory Repetition - Another method in furthering your development is to recite sentences and phrases aloud during your meditation. This is almost like a chant, and with your mind in an open, calm state, these life altering statements will sink even deeper into your mind.

Meditation can be used for anything, for becoming relaxed, to running through a match that's coming up, practicing for a rank advancement test, you name it! It is a powerful augmentation exercise for any martial artist, athlete or professional. This type of meditation can help you run through anything in your mind; correct mistakes that could be possible and help you realize the correct action and anchor it into your mind.

Mental Sparring

Mental sparring is a process in which you conduct a sparring match in your mind. There are various ways to do this. In mental sparring you're only controlling yourself consciously and let your subconscious mind take care of your opponent or opponents. It's all done from a first person perspective. You simply react to whatever comes at you. Before you begin pre-establish conditions in your mind. This allows your mind to know what to throw at you.

An advanced form of this exercise is to just let whatever happens happen. By not pre-establishing conditions it helps build up your reflexes and take down the shock of surprise in the real world.

Here's what your Mental Sparring should look like. Follow this step by step.
- In your mind start by setting the stage; an *infinite battlefield*, stretching as far as the eye can see. It can be anything from a landscape, building structure, or a simple wire frame (for me a wire frame environment was the easiest to establish first and then I moved up).
- You must be in a *first person view* (you can go to third person, but it's not as effective).
- The opponent appears and either you or they can *initiate the battle*.
- Focus on *performing your techniques*, if you have to, slow it down. However work up to speeds not attainable in real life.

- Feel in your mind your *muscles moving* as you are performing techniques (this activates the firing mechanism in your brain that links your muscles and your thought together).
- You're in a virtual world, so *anything is possible*, terrain can change, obstacles appear, opponents fade in and out of the battle.

If you want to work out a certain situation, lay it out in your mind, focus on doing what you know you should do, if you mess up correct it immediately.

Mental sparring is wonderful because it allows you to train and apply techniques in an almost real world situation. Your mind doesn't completely recognize what's real (The physical world) and what's not (in your mind). Everything is reality to it, thus mental sparring can give you almost real world experience without the danger of going out looking for someone to practice on the street. However it's not a complete substitute but it does help you improve greatly.

There are various ways to "Mental Spar". You can do it virtually anywhere! You can be mental sparring while you're on your run (one good reason to do this is it takes your mind off the run and puts it on something else). It can be done while meditating (as mentioned earlier in the chapter). You can be mental sparring while on the bus, in a line at the grocery store, in the car (although I don't recommend it while driving, you don't want to cause any accidents). The list is endless. One defining principle of when to do this exercise is, whenever you have free time and you're not thinking about something else, Mental Spar. On a side note, for any of you working on overcoming an addiction Mental Sparring can help. You're shifting your mind in a positive constructive area.

After applying this in my life I've seen a great deal of improvement. My skill and form seemed to improve drastically – why? I did it in my mind first, setting a foundation for the physical manifestation of the technique or combinations. Mental Sparring gets your mind right, and when done consistently it's a powerful accompaniment to physical training.

Trance Development

In order to build your ability to trance you have to practice. Here's what you do:

- Clear you mind.
- Take deep breaths and start to put yourself in a meditative state. Don't go all the way into meditation – just get yourself relaxed.
- Once your mind is clear go over your desired statements, say them in your mind (close your eyes to make this more powerful).
- Repeat them over and over; it's helpful to do one statement at a time for each exercise. Recite each statement anywhere from 20 to 100 times.
- At your last statement with all the energy of your soul open your eyes and declare your statement aloud with fervor.

This last step is powerful because for the previous 19 or 99 statements you've been reaffirming the statement to yourself, and in this last you're declaring it to the world with conviction and power. This adds greater belief in the statement you are incorporating into yourself.

Mind Expansion

Mind expansion is a process that expands your consciousness from beyond your physical body, a concept related to remote viewing. It can also be called Mind Projection by some (however word projection gives it a limited target place, rather than an area like we will discuss). The basic idea is to expand your field of thought around you, and eventually throughout the room you're in.

The Basic Process of developing Mind Expansion:
- Put yourself in a meditative state and focus on an area in your body.
- Move your consciousness from one point to another in your body (you do this by focusing on a specific area, like 'moving yourself there').
- The next step is to start to move your field of thought to the areas around you.

Projection is a good start, but it's not the end result you're looking for. You want a field of thought, an area around you that enables you to feel every movement within that field. If a punch or kick comes through it you feel it. You know in your mind its distance from your body, the speed its traveling at and the projected impact point (now this sounds like a complicated computer system, and luckily you have one – your brain) all calculated and given solutions for a counter attack. You feel everything in this area; emotions, another's presence, and any movement.

After you are proficient in projecting your consciousness, start expanding it as a field around and beyond your body.

- Start by focusing on as many areas of your body as possible. This develops the skill needed to put your consciousness in various places in and outside of your body.
- Once you can focus on all or almost all parts of your body start focusing on the ground you're standing on and the air immediately around your person.
- Keep pushing, increasing an inch or two at a time.

This type of exercise can't be measured in progress; it differs from one person to another. I've seen individuals that have taken a few months and some that struggle with it for years. This is a hard concept for some people to grasp. That in itself is one of their stumbling blocks. Some might classify this as a start to an "Omni-presence".

The results vary, from seeing solutions in your mind and choosing a reaction, simply reacting in a super human way, sensing a hit coming like a knife cutting through butter, or seeing the area around you in your mind.

Disclaimer, this exercise is in no way related to any physical substance. The results of these exercises are from pure development of the mind

Chapter Eight
Supplemental Exercises

"Without training one will never progress."

Earlier we talked about the need to control your emotions, and here are some exercises to accomplish that, along with other exercises and training methods to help you progress along this great quest. Emotional control comes through conditioning, experience in dealing with that emotion, taming the emotion to serve your purposes and desires and mental control.

Shadow Sparring

Another step beyond Mental Sparring is Shadow Sparring. Unlike Mental Sparring, with Shadow Sparring you're physically reacting. It helps to have a room large enough, or to be in a clear area. Just like Mental Sparring you let your mind come up with the opponent, you simply react.

You might think you're hallucinating, but you have to visualize something in front of you. You have to see the punches, the grapples and the kicks coming at you. Now if you're grappled or hit it won't physically affect you, but react in a way you normal would if it were real. You have enough time to defend or attack, your opponent is moving at a rate that your mind knows you can handle. Thus it's an easy way to build up speed and work on strategy. You're mind won't produce anything you can't handle.

I personally utilize shadow sparring frequently; it is part of my day to day routine. I suggest starting out anywhere from 5 to 10 minutes – keep it continuous, don't have any breaks in between. Now you can break it up into a few 5 minute segments, but it's a lot more effective if you have one continuous fight. Here's why;

- First off you build up stamina mentally and physically.
- Second you'll be able to keep up with any opponent out there.

- Third you have a continuous flow of technique which helps you learn how to blend every technique together.

Shadow Sparring is great to use on a punching bag. It really adds to the realness of a fight (mainly because you are making contact). As you spar with a bag keep your opponent right there, and if the bag is moving your opponent is moving with it. This is also a great way to practice aiming, timing and distance. Shadow Sparring can do wonders for improving your combat skills, and it's a great way to start preparing for those real life situations. In a way you're fostering a seed and you're helping it reach maturity by doing this kind of training, so that when the storms come that seed which is now a tree can stand on its on – *you* can stand on your own in a life or death situation.

Blind Fold Sparring

This type of sparring is phenomenal! It's all about building up your other senses, everything but sight is used here. Have you ever studied or talked to someone who was blind? Essentially all their other senses are heightened due to the lack of sight. In a way their senses become imbalanced. Their hearing is sharper, they can taste things more profoundly, their sense of smell is greater, and their touch is greatly enhanced. These are all great abilities right? Except you're blind. So this exercise is meant to help you gain these enhancements without losing your sight, permanently.

All you need is a partner, a clear safe room and a blind fold. Once you're blind folded you will have to sense where strikes are coming from

(this exercise is directly related to Mind Expansion). Some basic rules should be laid out for beginners in this type of exercise:
- No hitting in vital areas
- Strikes should be pulled to around 25% full force
- Start with single strikes and then build up
- You can play it out with the blind folded one being on defense only, and the one not blind folded on offense.

You need to take baby steps here to build things up. Gradually build up to full on sparring, and eventually both of you can be in blind folds (now that's when it gets crazy).

As you progress in your practice of this exercise you will be able to feel where your opponent is. Hear their movements, their cloths moving and muscles snapping into action. If you're on a patted mat or training ground you will feel their movements through the mat, due to the shift in mass within the mat. Mind Expansion enhances the natural progress that occurs when drilling this exercise and is a key component in truly mastering this type of training.

An adaptation of Mind Expansion is another option in this exercise. Once you're blind folded, expand your mind to the ground in the form of a web, by doing this you will be able to feel where your opponent is.

Night time sparring without light

Earlier in this book we shared an experience in how the ninja of Japan train to help control their emotional state. Sparring during the pitch black of night is one of the best ways to eliminate fear and calm your emotions in preparing for a real life situation. Here are some different ideas on how you can implement this into your training.

> **Sparring in your Own Acreage** - Depending on how many acres you or your family own, it can prove to be a valuable place for this type of training. Most large lots have a limited lighted area ideal for this type of exercise.
> Your own yard if surrounded by trees can be one of the best spots to train. It gives you obstacles and terrain to maneuver around and to use in strategy. If you do have obstacles large enough to conceal yourself it gives an additional element of surprise to help simulate the surprise in a real life situation.
>
> **Camp Sites** - If you train with a group of people locally and are close to camp sites you have another battlefield. Make sure that during the day time you mark out your area and clear it of any harmful obstacles that could cause serious wounds – you definitely don't want to have an accident out in the middle of nowhere. Make certain arrangements with local law enforcement to let them know about your training exercise, and nearby campers.
>
> **Personally owned** - Property that is personally owned by yourself or another party that sanctions this type of training is another great area. Make sure you have permission to be on the premises, and have any written material verifying the permission in case local law enforcement arrives. It helps when the person owning the property is there too.

Areas to avoid - Local parks are not areas to have sparring matches at night. Most public places not lit at night can be used for illegal activity. Schools and Churches are also areas to avoid. You don't want to confuse yourselves with any illegal activity.

The advantages to this type of sparring include:
- One, you get to improve other senses, much like in Blind Fold Sparring exercises.
- Two, you get to experience the emotions of surprise, suspense, fear, and other emotions.
- Three, you build your ability to fight in an area you don't recognize.

One final note about this 'Night Training – You must keep it fresh. If you do not change the environment it will become rote and stale. Emotions will not be stimulated; it will be a 'dead' exercise. Remember when things are new and unexpected the true character and abilities of the warrior emerges.

Iron Shirt Training a.k.a. Pain Tolerance Training

The ability to control and deal with pain can go a long way in a real world fight, or even some competitions. The idea behind pain tolerance exercises are to build up your ability to function under pain, and deal with fear. If you can tolerate pain, what is there left to fear? The ability to tolerate pain shows in your countenance and is a powerful tool in psychological combat.

The idea of Iron Shirt training has been around for centuries. Some oriental disciplines require this type of training as essential in your growth as a martial artist. The concept of Iron Shirt is to make your skin tough like Iron. Your skin can't be iron, but you can train yourself to be like iron in resisting blows, as if it didn't faze you. It's an incredible tool. Imagine, how you would feel fighting an opponent who could not feel pain? Wouldn't that cause a little fear, and perhaps hopelessness? There are various methods of achieving this iron body and we'll outline some basic training you can undergo right now without any special equipment.

Hot & Cold - The extreme shift from hot to cold inflicts a great deal of pain. There are quite a few methods one can use. One of the easiest and the one I recommend to use is your own shower.

- Warm the shower; find a temperature you feel comfortable with.
- After you're soaked turn it as cold as you can, not too much (remember we're starting out and you don't want to have a heart attack).
- Make the shift from hot to cold several times.
- Once you start to build your tolerance go as far as you can on either side of the spectrum.

This is such a simple exercise to do and it takes hardly any time, you're going to shower anyway, why not add some training to it? This is a great exercise, because it ranges in temperature. You can start out as a beginner and advance with just this one exercise. It's the best way to fully train your entire body.

There are additional ways of applying this Hot & Cold concept. One might have a large pot of boiling water and another of ice water, alternating punches from one to the other. Another substitute for the hot water is an open flame.

Fire Exposure - A variant of Hot & Cold is sole Fire Exposure. Mainly used for training your arms, but can be applied to other areas of the body. A candle is the best tool; meditation helps greatly, so I suggest undergoing meditation first before this exercise. Make sure you have a regular candle, ones in a jar don't work well for what we want to do, also don't use a scent unless you plan on using that scent to activate any mindset associated with your Iron Shirt.

- Light the candle.
- Move your hand as close as possible (if you have hair on your hands it's going to sting and stink until you burn them all off, which might be after a couple runs with this exercise).
- Bathe your hand in the heat, holding each area of your hand or arm (e.g. palm and top of the hand) for ten seconds for a start. Ideally you want to build up the length of time in the flame.
- You can alternate hands if the pain is too much to bathe one hand consecutively.
- Three to five minutes is an excellent amount of time to start out with.

A variation of this exercise is to bathe your forearms. One reason why we do this is to strength our blocking and parrying areas. Be careful especially if you have a lot of hair on your arms, I suggest trimming or even shaving your arms when doing this exercise.

Some extremes of Fire Exposure training are a tad radical and can resemble self mutilation. We don't encourage any of this activity. We will look over some ideas and discuss why it's used to strengthen one's body.

- **Torch Training.** This exercise requires multiple persons, and can be extremely dangerous. A torch is lit and used to bathe the body of the practitioner. The body undergoes much of the same reaction your hand would; it makes the skin tougher, plus the extreme stinging in various areas of the body act as a tool to develop tolerance to weapons and other forms of pain inflicting objects.
- **Hot Coals.** These exercises have been used by various spiritualists, and martial artists. Some of the more famous incidents have been of spiritual leaders laying on hot coals, or walking across the coals. This form of heat tolerance gives a constant steady burning that can make one numb to the pain.

Training on Hard Ground - One of the best ways to build up the strength in one's skin is to do various training on a hard surface like concrete. Knuckle Push Ups are wonderful on concrete. Training Bare foot on concrete strengthens one's feet, and builds up resistance to pain, especially when you land from jumping or lunging. Training rolls and other ground exercises on concrete or asphalt help to simulate actual combat and prepare you for the actual thing (you might get some cuts and scrapes but hey, better to get them in training than in an actual fight).

I recommend training on hard ground when you've learned and mastered it on the mat. The hard surface is the next step in your progression.

Everyday Training - Having a mindset of training anywhere anytime can create unlimited opportunities to further develop yourself. For instance, one might do a type of fire training while washing dishes by hand. If you have a dishwasher ditch it and go the old fashion way. The secret to this type of heat training is to turn up the water as hot as possible. Much like your dishwasher, the faucet will pump out the heat to clean the dishes and strengthen your hands. Depending on how many people live with you you'll get in a good training and clean dishes. Realistically you can get anywhere from 5 to 20 minutes worth of pain tolerance training, and if you're on a tight schedule this might be one of the few times you can work on this type of exercise.

Pain Tolerance isn't a practice used in many martial arts in the west. Perhaps it comes with a brutal notion attached to it, or an unethical way of life. Whatever the opinion, pain tolerance helps you progress. It increases your ability to control your emotions, provides additional room for growth in the arts and allows you to master yourself more fully.

Emotional Control

Emotional Control in combat is crucial. Your emotions determine your physiological state. This state has to be in perfect balance in order to win a match or survive a fight. Whenever a person becomes emotionally unstable in a fight a couple things happen; they start to lose control in their precision to execute techniques, their mind becomes blurred and they begin to lose their discipline, in essence reverting back to an animalistic state. It's like going back to phase one we talked about earlier in the "Three steps to perfection" in Chapter Two.

We have outlined various exercises throughout this book that show how to balance your emotions. I'll give you a couple exercises that are directly focused on this subject.

> **Visualization** - During a visualization session, or during your meditation, it is good to conjure up images in your mind of areas you feel you are emotionally weak in. For instance, if you get nervous when you're ganged up on in the street or becoming overwhelmed in the final round of the upcoming tournament. Perhaps you dread walking alone at night. Whatever the circumstance may be, simulate it in your mind. Hold it there and tame the emotions swelling within you. Harness them, control them – all the while keeping the image vivid and in front of you.

> **Fear Confrontation** - One of the best ways to learn how to handle your emotions is to face it straight on. There are various ways to do this. Going to the place of your fears, standing there and soaking it all in. One of my favorites is what we call an "Arrow Break". It's a wonderful way to face and overcome your fears. The arrow break is an extremely powerful training technique –

however it can be dangerous without the proper supervision of an experienced professional.

Controlled Thought - As we mentioned in Chapter Four, thoughts influence our emotions and our physiological state. You must identify the emotions you wish to build for a fight. Outline each one and associate thoughts or mental images that trigger that emotional response. Each mind is different and you are the only one who knows your mind, so reach in, dig deeper and pull out the thoughts, the words or the images that invoke your desired emotions. Once you have those thoughts down, focus on them at least once a day. You must get your mind into the habit of focusing on these thoughts in normal controlled situations to make these emotions a part of you.

> "The man who controls his thoughts controls his world"
> - Robert Zangari

Emotional balance is one of the pinnacle heights one can reach in self mastery, not just in martial arts but every aspect of life. Being able to remain calm in other types of situations is a good first step, but that doesn't compare to a fight. You won't have the same rush of emotions when asking a girl out on a date for the first time, or speaking in public. These produce emotions that can cloud judgment and skill, but it won't be to the caliber of your emotions in a fight. On the flip side when you're able to control your emotional state in a fight, the rest of life is like a cake walk.

Chapter Nine
The Final Capstone

"Martial Art is to become, not to do."

There is a secret that enables one to reach their fullest potential. It is a secret that channels the Warrior Spirit within and magnifies it over a thousand fold. This secret is the standard of Moral Conduct, a Code of Honor, a Standard of Actions and Beliefs and more importantly living by them.

The Standard, the Code

You must be a cause of Defense; defending yourself, your family, your rights and privileges, your way of life. A *righteous* cause empowers us to do things not normally possible. In order for you to excel in Martial Arts you must have a driving cause, a 'why you're doing this'. Having the right cause *empowers* you.

> **Righteous:** the act of following a Moral obligation or a Standard.

At RZD Academy of Martial Arts & Life we promote a code of honor. This code is the basis of our conduct. It is the Law that we adhere to as Martial Artists. This code is similar to the Mantra found at the beginning of Chapter Six, but it is separate from it. The first was a list to identify attributes that make up the Ultimate Warrior, an ever building collection of principles and attributes you can take upon yourself throughout your life. The Code of Honor is a law, a list of standards of righteousness. Every human being recognizes that these points of honor are 'good' and uplifting. It is built within us to seek after these things, and through Martial Arts we can find them and apply them.

"I defend the innocent, the weak – those who cannot defend themselves. I intervene when possible against the acts of Evil. I am a Shield to those around me. I do not tolerate injustice, I uphold the Laws of the Land I abide in. I am an ally of Truth and Justice. I will not tolerate the suffering of others, and I will do all in my power to ease their troubles. I do not start conflict; I defuse conflict that comes my way. I respect the lives of others. I do not take that which does not belong to me, unless it is first offered. I am giving and considerate to all those around me. I am kind and generous to those around me who are in need. I am tender with the people and things around me, I restrain my full power. I do not use my power and ability for ill use, only for the betterment of those around me. I am honest in all my dealings with others. I cultivate continual hope. I finish anything I start; I am diligent to the end. I am consistent in all things and pace myself so that I can finish what I start. I am self reliant; I do what I can myself before relying on others. I have morally clean thoughts. I am loyal to my family, the standards of my upbringing and to those I have agreed to do business with. I am a gentleman or a lady, I act with chivalry. Deception is a tool only used in combat; it is not suited for everyday life. I am patient in my dealings with others and myself. I take time to evaluate and reassess the situation I am currently in. I am grateful at all times, and when despair, depression, anger, sorrow and grief appear I shift my focus to gratitude. I love others. I show a genuine concern for their well being. I think of others first and put their needs above my wants. Love is the attribute that governs my life, I do everything with love."

Attributes and Personal Characteristics

There are a list of Attributes, Characteristics and Actions one must possess and do. We will cover a majority of them here, there are more and it would fill volumes of books to talk about all these things – but we will cover the main or central attributes that all of them stem from.

Who you are shapes the world around you. What you are determines your decisions, your habits, your lifestyle, your friends, your surroundings. If you want to change where you are now you have to change WHAT you are.

How does one change? Is it the changing of actions? The changing of attitude? The changing of environment? Or the changing of thoughts? All of these in some degree have an influence on your newly changed self. Actions can result in a change of attitude and thought, but it does not ensure change. Attitude is one of the larger factors in change, but there are also additional elements. Environment has the advantage of a 'fresh start'. You are able to create a thought pattern or habits more easily. However environment is not the complete solution. Thoughts are the root of change. When you change your thoughts the rest of your life begins to change and mold itself to your thoughts. Unless the defining element is included even your thoughts will not be able to permanently change your life.

Choice is the *defining element* in change. You must exercise your ability to choose to change. All of these areas are great starts, but without a conscious and subconscious desire and determination to change, fueled by choice you will not permanently change. In developing attributes and characteristics choice is the *igniter*. The ability to choose is the greatest gift you possess. *Use* it to better yourself.

The main attributes and characteristics we will discuss are as follows; Righteousness, Virtue, Honesty, Loyalty, Benevolence, Patience, Diligence, Courage, Hope, Faith, Obedience, Kindness, Tenderness, Love, Gratitude, and Respect. We will outline what each of these mean, but first here is an activity for you.

EXERCISE
Write down a brief definition about what you think each of these are and then, let us compare answers. Identify any additional information and add it to your list.

>**Righteousness** - Unwavering diligence to all that is good, wholesome and worthwhile. Righteousness is an attribute that when possessed others fall into place. It is to be honorable in words and in deeds. In essence, you possess all these attributes and more. It is a Characteristic that all great and noble warriors possess.
>
>**Virtue** - Is cleanliness in our thoughts and actions. To test your virtue one must merely look into the inner most parts of their mind. To have Virtue is to have a mind that is clear of confusion, strictly uphold the Laws of the Universe, and acts upon those thoughts of cleanliness.
>
>**Honesty** - To have truth in all things associated with you. Honesty is not just being honest in your words, but your everyday actions

and your associations. However some of us can be too Honest at time, therefore wisdom and honesty are the best mingled together. People do not need to know the details but the point you are conveying.

Loyalty - When there is unwavering devotedness there is Loyalty. To Live and Die for a cause is to be loyal. To defend every ideal that makes up your being is loyalty not only to yourself but to those principles and attributes that shape you. Loyalty and honesty are intertwined in relationships; they are what truly make up friendship. Loyalty is honesty and dedication to a higher cause.

Benevolence - The acts of Righteousness, the attribute that drives you to help those in need, defend those around you. The force inside you that radiates, "I will not stand for evil!" To be Benevolent is to act righteous and good.

Patience - "You must have the patience of water". Like water we must be patient in every aspect of life. Patience is the ability to see the end result and stay focused in the here and now. Patience and Time overcome all, and for the warrior who is patient victory is achieved. Patience is timing.

Diligence - Like a mountain stream, the one who is Diligent is always moving forward. It is consistency and persistence. To be Diligent is to be Patient and hard working toward your goals. The warrior who is Diligent in their training will obtain the skills, abilities, and results they desire. "Rome was not built in a day" and neither are you.

Courage - The ability to face fear and push through it. Courage is not just overwhelming valor, but the determination to see through the little fears in life. Yes, I mean to call some fears little because they are. The fear of making a phone call, applying for a certain job, asking the girl of your dreams out on a date, or even the fear of doing the little things such as saying "I love you" or a simple smile to a saddened soul. Courage is to conquer fear not destroy it. The fear still exists; we merely act in spite of it. Everyone has fears some of us just *chose* to just ignore or tame them.

Hope - Hope is to want something, some result or someone. Hope is what gets the seed of desire planted within us. It is the initial spark. It is what captures the imagination. In order to continually grow we must have hope. When we reach new heights in our development we must cultivate new hope. The hope of being able to train for five hours a day is gone when you are able to maintain that same training routine. Therefore new hope must be made in order to grow.

Faith - Faith is the ability to see things that are not presently here, but we know they are true. Faith is an overwhelming sense of belief in someone or something. Faith vanquishes doubt and disbelief. With Perfect Faith one can get through anything. To have faith in your abilities is crucial in any training or competition, and more especially in a street fight. Faith is an underlying principle in life. Faith is also action, to act upon the things we believe in. Faith is not "Yeah I can throw ten punches per second", it is throwing those ten punches and knowing you could do it all along. Faith is confidence in yourself or someone else. Faith is to put your trust in someone or something. Ultimately it is to Trust and Act.

Obedience - In order to be obedient there must be a law or a standard given. As Martial Artists it is our privilege and duty to obey our Masters, our Codes of Honor, our Personal Standards, and to the Standards of Universal Moral Conduct. When we are obedient righteousness follows. Obedience to the Laws of the Universe brings the results we are looking for. Through obedience we reach the Third and Final stage of development.

Kindness - The outward manifestation of Charity, or pure love. Kindness is shown after the battle. To be kind we show mercy to our opponents after sure victory is obtained. It is an outward manifestation of whether we are "good" or "evil". After the battle we allow our opponent's to live, and if necessary invite and incise them to change for the better. Kindness is shown after strength and victory.

Tenderness - "To be hard yet soft". In all of our movements as a martial artist we must be hard and soft. Tenderness is to have consideration for the opponent, not to feel sorry, but to be aware of bodily limits. But beyond combat and training, tenderness for all things around us is crucial. It is the harnessing of strength, knowing there is power to cripple your enemy yet restraining it. To be tender is to show you are in control of yourself.

Love - To have pure love is to reach ultimate excellence. In order to possess this, a conscious effort must play a role in every action and every word. Love is *alive*, it is fresh, and it is ever moving like water. Pure love is to act with the other person's best interests in mind. Love is *selflessness*. We abandon the petty "what I want" and focus on "what do they need?" Sometimes when we are in a situation between life and death, and the other person wants us dead or desires to injure us, this is not the answer. But rather how can I keep myself alive and defuse this situation.
Love has a powerful effect on the world around us. It is one of the greatest attributes one can possess on this earth.

Gratitude - Gratitude is not just thankfulness but happiness, overwhelming happiness. It is joy for the things which we have. Gratitude washes away sadness and despair. It helps us get back on track and refocus our energy. To be grateful is one of the greatest gifts one can possess, because it opens the gates of opportunity to us, and enables us to receive more. Not with the intent to seek more, but with the intent that we love and are thankful for what we have right now, this instant and where it all came from. Just a mere shift in our thoughts can develop gratitude and change your day. Gratitude is a conscious effort, and when it becomes a habit then it is a subconscious effort.

Respect - is the ability to retain ourselves, to refrain from yielding to our natural negative selves when interacting with others and ourselves. To Respect ourselves is a form of Obedience to the Laws and Standards we have agreed to. We Respect our bodies by training them and giving them proper food and nourishment. Respect to others is to be Honest and Loyal, Kind and Tender. Respect is an outward sign of Virtue and Righteousness.

When one lives and becomes these attributes they grant power and enable you to do things far beyond what you could comprehend. They empower you to do the impossible. You bring down the powers of the Universe to aid you and you can accomplish, if you will, whatever is just and true.

MARTIAL ARTS: Ultimate Warrior

Conclusion

Martial Arts are about growth. Growth of yourself, helping those around you grow and growing the community you live in. There are countless exercises one can do, new ones appearing every day. This is a simple list you can start with. We implement all these and more at RZD Academy of Martial Arts & Life. We believe there are limitless possibilities for expanding the mind, body and spirit.

The way a martial artist trains is a direct reflection of their entire life. If you change the way you train you change the way you live. You must train in a way of ultimate excellence, growing and achieving new heights every day. It is about what you can do, not what you can't do. If you can't do all or any of the exercises in this book that's fine! You can start out small and work your way up. You can't climb to the top of the ladder from the middle; you have to start at the bottom.

We've shared many important aspects in this book, some will be life changing and you will never be the same again. Remember, you're always progressing, this is an endless journey, and you're on it. There will always be people around you supporting you and lifting you up, you might not see them, but they're there even if they're hundreds or even thousands of miles away. By reading and applying this book you've already taken the steps necessary to help you gain that achievement of the most powerful warrior. May you be strengthened in your quest and achieve what *you* desire in life. I am grateful for the time you have spent reading and applying the knowledge in this book, "Thank you", it has been a pleasure. I hope you prosper in all your doings, in the Arts and outside of them. You are on a wonderful journey, and our paths will meet again. Until then, farewell.

MARTIAL ARTS: Ultimate Warrior

Here are links to…

This Book's Website
www.MartialArtsUltimateWarrior.com.

Books
www.Martial-Arts-Bookstore.com Visit our Bookstore for a list of additional books by the author and other Martial Artists.

Products
www.Martial-Arts-RZDAcademy.com/Store/Products Visit for a products mentioned in this book and others.

Affiliate Program
www.Martial-Arts-RZDAcademy.com/Affiliate. Liked the book and want to share it with others? Get paid to do so! Earn 5%-25% on products and courses when you Join our Affiliate Program. No cost to join, no membership fees, no annual fees, absolutely FREE of cost to you!

RZD Academy of Martial Arts & Life
www.Martial-Arts-RZDAcademy.com. Our Homepage, be sure to bookmark it!

Course Information
www.Martial-Arts-RZDAcademy.com/Courses. Visit for a list of current and future courses. Sign up today for your FREE Trial.

Long Distance Training Programs
www.Martial-Arts-RZDAcademy.com/HomeStudy visit for details on our long distance study programs, Remember each book comes with a FREE Introductory course, no obligation to continue and 100%, 30 Day Money Back Guarantee after the end of your FREE Course.

Ryu Zangari Do®

Send in for your FREE Introductory Course outlining the basics of RZD Academy of Martial Arts & Life's flag ship course, Ryu Zangari Do®. In this program you will…

- Discover ways of *intergrading multiple styles* and *philosophies*,
- Learn *unique techniques*,
- Develop and Apply *Modernized Self Defense*, and
- Experience a host of Accelerated Learning Techniques.

Your FREE Introductory Course will give you a glimmer into the world of RZD and start you on an epic journey.

Ryu Zangari Do is founded on the principles of Jeet Kune Do, Ninjutsu (Togakure-Ryu), Wing Chun Gung Fu, Karate and modern combat. It respects all the traditions of each school and offers unique ways of combining these influential disciplines into one encompassing system of combat.

To *claim* your FREE course simply…

Email the information below to FreeCourse.RZDAcademy@comcast.net
Or cut and mail this form to our Headquarters *

```
Name _____

Address _____ Apt_____
City _____ State_____ Zip _____
Phone Number _____
Email: _____

           Validation Code: 978345
```

* Your personal information will never be shared with any third party or outside source. Current address located at www.MartialArtsUltimateWarrior.com/Contact.html

Bibliography

Hayes, S. K. (1981). *The Ninja and their secret fighting art.* Tokyo, Japan: Charles E. Tuttle Company.

Lee, B. (1997). *Bruce Lee, The Art of Expressing the Human Body* (Vol. Four). (J. Little, Ed.) North Clarendon, Vermont, USA: Charles E. Tuttle Co.

Minford, J. (2002). *The Art of War.* New York: Penguin Group.

Index

A

Accelerated, 10, 21, 62
Agility, 25, 54
Aikido, 41
Anime, 41
Antioxidant, 52, 80
Attitude, 36, 114, 121, 136, 164

B

Battlefield, 11, 16, 31, 58, 71, 88, 91, 92, 93, 96, 104, 116, 117, 129, 131, 143, 153
Benevolence, 165, 166
Blind Fold Sparring, 151, 154
Block, 14, 28, 42, 51, 90, 91, 92, 123, 125, 126
Body, 26, 29, 36, 39, 47, 50, 51, 54, 61, 62, 65, 66, 69, 71, 74, 76, 79, 80, 81, 84, 88, 89, 93, 115, 121, 124, 126, 130, 132, 134, 137, 138, 140, 146, 147, 155, 156, 157, 171
Book, 9, 10, 13, 16, 46, 47, 50, 57, 61, 74, 89, 91, 101, 107, 111, 130, 131, 141, 152, 159, 171, 172
Boxing, 37, 130
Breakfast, 74, 76
Broken Rhythm, 38, 39

C

Callisthenic, 54
Cardiovascular, 50, 55
Chicken, 51, 75, 77
Choice, 52, 75, 77, 79, 90, 115, 116, 137, 164
Combat, 46, 58, 89, 91, 96, 99, 104, 106, 111, 116
Combination, 35, 38, 42, 52, 67, 112, 127
Courage, 165, 167

D

Deception, 31, 32, 37, 38, 163
Defense, 16, 27, 28, 40, 59, 91, 114, 162
Deflection, 89
Diet, 51, 66
Diligence, 165, 166
Dinner, 75, 77
Dojo, 13, 14, 15, 16, 17, 18, 60, 123

E

Emotion, 15, 16, 82, 84, 95, 124, 150
Environment, 17, 29, 30, 57, 91, 107, 108, 143, 164
Evil, 86, 88, 113, 166, 168

F

Faith, 165, 167
Fear, 16, 18, 20, 36, 58, 86, 87, 96, 99, 113, 117, 118, 152, 154, 155, 167
Fighting, 8, 12, 13, 15, 16, 19, 28, 34, 38, 40, 49, 59, 69, 82, 92,

MARTIAL ARTS: Ultimate Warrior
101, 104, 109, 111, 113, 114, 117, 124, 127, 130, 131, 137, 138, 155

Firm Wits, 25

Fish, 51, 75, 77, 80

Fist, 32, 43, 97, 116

Fitness, 49, 50, 65, 67, 74

Flame, 156

Flexibility, 15, 38, 53, 67, 68, 72, 74, 127

Fruit, 75, 76

G

Goal, 21, 74, 83, 99, 108, 111, 133, 134, 141

Good, 37, 73

Grapple, 41, 57, 68, 98, 125, 142

Gratitude, 165, 169

Gypsies, 95

H

Hand, 20, 21, 29, 31, 32, 43, 51, 55, 69, 72, 73, 89, 90, 99, 107, 117, 122, 136, 156, 157, 158

Hayes, 16, 32

Heat, 156, 157, 158

Honesty, 165

Hope, 165, 167

I

In-Combat Brainwashing, 46, 58, 89, 91, 96, 99, 111

Iron determination, 25

Iron Shirt, 154, 156

Isometric, 54

Isotonic, 54

J

Jeet Kune Do, 8, 28, 49, 53, 118, 122, 134

Jujutsu, 117

K

Karate, 8, 28

Kata, 13, 60

Kenjutsu, 8

Kiai, 41

Kiap, 41, 42, 43, 44, 45

Kick, 14, 18, 26, 28, 33, 35, 39, 42, 75, 96, 104, 105, 115, 116, 119, 123, 125, 127, 146

Kindness, 165, 168

Kotodama, 40, 88, 113

L

Lee, 15, 27, 38, 49, 52

Love, 78, 87, 110, 163, 167, 168, 169

Love, 163, 165, 169

Loyalty, 165, 166

Lunch, 75, 76

M

Maintain, 49, 167

Martial Arts, 8, 10, 12, 13, 16, 19, 20, 41, 47, 50, 53, 60, 66, 67, 74, 86, 122, 123, 124, 125, 137, 162, 171, 172

Master, 14, 32, 35, 49, 62, 105, 131, 158

MARTIAL ARTS: Ultimate Warrior
Mastery, 58, 60
Meat, 76, 77, 80
Mental, 10, 27, 34, 36, 41, 45, 46, 47, 59, 82, 88, 91, 94, 96, 97, 100, 101, 109, 112, 115, 118, 120, 124, 143, 144, 160
Mind, 10, 12, 13, 14, 18, 19, 20, 21, 24, 25, 26, 27, 29, 30, 36, 37, 39, 40, 42, 46, 47, 48, 59, 60, 61, 62, 65, 83, 84, 86, 87, 88, 89, 90, 91, 92, 93, 94, 95, 96, 97, 98, 99, 100, 104, 108, 109, 110, 113, 115, 120, 124, 128, 129, 130, 131, 132, 133, 134, 137, 138, 139, 140, 141, 142, 143, 144, 145, 146, 147, 150, 152, 159, 160, 165, 169, 171
Mind expansion, 146
Mindset, 18, 37, 43, 46, 111, 129
Muscle, 81

N

Ninjutsu, 8, 32
Nitric Oxide, 79

O

Obedience, 165, 168
Offense, 42, 152
Offensive defense, 28
Omega 3, 80

P

Pain Tolerance, 154, 158
Parries, 69, 117
Parry, 14, 42, 60
Patience, 165, 166
Power, 24, 25, 26, 36, 40, 41, 42, 49, 69, 70, 82, 86, 104, 105, 127, 130, 133, 141, 145, 163, 169, 170
Projection, 41, 87, 93, 94, 95, 146
Punch, 14, 17, 18, 28, 32, 33, 35, 39, 42, 43, 44, 59, 60, 69, 71, 91, 97, 104, 105, 112, 115, 116, 119, 120, 122, 125, 127, 146

R

Religion, 41
Resistance, 30, 54, 55, 68, 157
Respect, 165, 170
Rice, 51, 74, 75, 76, 77
Righteousness, 165
Ryu Zangari Do, 8

S

Science, 123
Secret, 61
Self Defense, 12, 42, 92, 113, 114, 115
Spar, 19, 24, 55, 151
Sparring, 14, 17, 18, 28, 33, 35, 38, 39, 40, 42, 44, 45, 47, 48, 50, 60, 70, 104, 113, 115, 122, 123, 133, 138, 142, 143, 144, 150, 151, 152, 154
Speed, 10, 25, 27, 29, 30, 35, 54, 55, 60, 61, 68, 69, 71, 84, 97, 126, 130, 146, 150
Spiritual, 10, 40, 41, 109, 157
Story, 16, 30, 49, 50, 53, 82, 96, 118

MARTIAL ARTS: Ultimate Warrior

Strategy, 24, 39, 97, 104, 108, 111, 114, 115, 116, 119, 122, 123, 124, 125, 127, 130, 150, 153
Strength training, 54
Stress, 54, 118
Student, 14, 16, 61, 62
Styles, 13, 14, 19, 21, 24, 28, 38, 40, 106, 115, 116, 122, 123, 125
Sun Tzu, 24, 31, 34, 44, 107
Supplements, 52, 79
Surroundings, 106, 164
Survival, 37, 88
System, 8, 51, 83, 122, 123, 146

T

Tactics, 61, 106, 121
Tae Kwan Do, 28, 122
Tame, 16, 87, 89, 159
Technique, 40, 41, 44, 45, 49, 62, 68, 72, 74, 91, 96, 100, 104, 117, 145, 151, 159
Tenderness, 165, 168
Thoughts, 18, 26, 86, 87, 88, 89, 90, 93, 94, 95, 96, 97, 98, 101, 140, 160, 163, 164, 165, 169

Tocopherols, 80
Tocotrinels, 80
To-Shin-Do, 8

U

Ultimate, 21, 87, 130, 131, 132, 162

V

Victory, 12, 18, 27, 31, 36, 37, 86, 88, 89, 97, 99, 107, 123, 130, 166, 168
Virtue, 165, 170
Visualization, 62, 133, 141, 159
Voice, 40, 41, 42, 43, 44, 45, 58, 84, 92, 113, 136

W

War, 24, 99, 107, 130
Water, 78
Weight, 29, 30, 50, 54, 55, 56, 69, 70, 71, 77, 82, 84, 121
Wild Alaskan, 51
Wing Chun, 8, 122
Words, 41, 86, 88, 93

www.ingramcontent.com/pod-product-compliance
Lightning Source LLC
Chambersburg PA
CBHW020949230426
43666CB00005B/236